Toff Down Pit

KIT FRASER

LARGE PRINT

Oxford, England

British Library Cataloguing in Publication Data
Fraser, Kit
  Toff Down Pit. – New ed
  I. Title
  622.334092

622.33
888752

ISBN 1-85695-137-5

Printed and bound by Hartnolls Ltd, Bodmin, Cornwall

Thanks to Nicholas Monson
for his editing

Dedicated to Sarah

GLOSSARY OF MINING TERMS

bait = snack

bank = surface; **on bank** = on the surface

bull = large girder used to stop runaway trams

bunker = open-top tank

button, the pulling and pushing of which stops and starts motors which run conveyor belts, endless haulage ropes and tuggers

cage = pitman's lift

canch = stone wall left standing once coal has been extracted from the heading of a tunnel. Usually is cleared away by shotfiring

cavil = authorized place of work

chocknob = short oblong bit of wood

chocks = used at coalface to keep roof up. Has replaced old pit prop

chumming = empty tram

clip = metal contraption which is used to connect tram to endless conveyor belt, upon which coal is transported from coalface to shaft

datal = most junior

dac = tannoy

dog = nail used to pin rail to sleeper

doubler = two consecutive shifts

dowell = to drill with hickory stick at coalface in order to support crumbly roof

drift = most spacious roadway

development worker makes tunnels

endless = circular haulage rope

fault = displacement of coal seam by layer of stone

firedamp = methane gas

goaf = what is left after coal has been extracted from coalface

hack = pick

heading = the end of a tunnel, in the process of being worked

heap = place where pitmen assemble prior to going down in the cage

heavy = steep incline

hedgehog = tangled ball in endless

hickory stick = wooden pole used for dowelling

inbye = in direction of coalface

inchboard = inch-thick plank of wood

intake air = air going inbye

kist = container of tools and equipment

machine = shearer

manset = underground train

mell = huge hammer

Miner = machine used for tunnelling

mulligate = one of the two tunnels that lead to the face

onsetter = liftman

outbye = in direction of shaft

panzer = metal-face conveyor belt

powerloader = faceman or development worker

prop = roof support

pull-lift = chain and lever and axle contraption used for lifting heavy things

refuge hole = man-sized alcove in wall of tunnel

return air = air outbye

return wheel, through which endless is threaded. Two to an endless like two jagged wheels to a bicycle chain

roadway = tunnel used for travelling

rubs = tokens. Cf. **putting rubs in** = putting tokens in helmet. Pitman's way of doing Eeny Meeny Miny Mo

seam = layer of coal

selfix = tube of jelly-like glue

self-rescuer = tin box worn at pitman's belt. It contains an hour's worth of protection against carbon monoxide in the air

set = column of carriages or trams

shaft, up and down which the cage goes

sharp louse = early finish

shearer = machine used at the face to win the coal

sheckle = metal blob on haulage rope

shifter = adjustable spanner

shotfire = explode

slurry = sloppy coal muck

stageloader = machine which runs a short metal conveyor belt that takes coal off panzer and plonks it on first belt outbye

stonedust bag = like cement bag only half the weight and twice as comfortable to sit on

sylvester = contraption consisting of lever, comb and chain. Used for pulling out stubborn old pit props or tightening the tension on endless

timber = chocknobs, inchboards, crown props, barks, splits

wall = coalface

wedge = slim little piece of wood placed behind wheel

of stationary tram to prevent it slipping downhill

wet note = much coveted note signed by an official authorizing a financial reward (normally not more than 50p) for working in wet conditions

WALL

PANZER
(coalface conveyor belt)

SHEARER
(coalcutting machine)

MULLIGATE TUNNEL

TAILGATE TUNNEL

STAGELOADER

TRANSFORMER
(supplies electricity to coalface)

TELEPHONE TO CONTROL

CONVEYOR BELT

TRAM TRACKS
(materials for the coalface transported along these)

CUT COAL

GOAF
(area left where coal has been extracted)

INTRODUCTION

It was on the train journey to South Shields that I felt the bottom fall out of my stomach. This adventure could turn out to be a terrible mistake. Was it really so sensible interrupting my journalistic career to become a miner? Could I, a twenty-three-year-old toff, survive a week, never mind a year, hacking out coal in tunnels a thousand feet beneath the surface of the earth? And would my fellow pitmen tolerate someone different from themselves?

Probably not. But I had to try. It had been a whimsical idea at first but now I was dead set on it. I wanted to know whether I had what it took to be a coalminer. Past generations had wars to test their manhood. This was going to be my little battle.

But it wasn't just a vehicle for a personal challenge. There was also my curiosity. Was the job as tough or as dangerous as was popularly reckoned? Were the miners worth their wage demands? And what exactly was life like in a pit community?

Like much of the world, I suppose I was somewhat awed by the miners' fearsome ability to topple a Conservative government. So I also wanted to know if there really was "communist infiltration" in the union, as various Fleet Street headlines had proclaimed, or was this charge just tabloid hysteria? Being in a national strike, I hoped, would answer that.

From the point of view of my personal life, I felt I would almost certainly benefit from exposure to people radically different from myself — people whom I imagined live life in the raw. Until this juncture I had had the privilege of a sheltered existence — private schooling, a year in Paris learning French and three years as a reporter on a small Scottish paper, the *Galloway Gazette*.

In Paris a woman had called me a "Catholic virginal prig" and the remark still stung. I was hoping to redress whatever damage an exclusive public-school education had wreaked on my character. Perhaps pit life would also help me overcome my inhibitions. There was still my virginity to lose. These and other thoughts whirled in my mind as the train trundled south.

I had in fact been lucky to get the job at all, for various people had told me that getting into the coalmines was as difficult as getting into Eton. Apparently you have to have relations in the pit before you are even considered. So in my letter of application I had written that my grandfather had been a miner — which was truthful, though misleading. He had in fact been a goldminer in South Africa, where he managed Africans who did the manual work for him.

Actually, my acceptance owed more to timing than to my dubious credentials. An early retirement scheme had recently been announced by the NCB and replacements were suddenly needed after a sizeable exodus of miners taking advantage of redundancy cheques.

I had sent a letter off to the manpower department of the NCB in Gateshead saying that I had A-levels and that

I was not a Trotskyist, that mining was the career for me and that I wanted to start from the bottom and work my way up. I received a reply saying that at the moment there was not a vacancy but that my name would be considered should one crop up within the next couple of months.

I was still waiting when one day I noticed a full-page advertisement in the *Sun* newspaper, exhorting readers to become coalminers. Anybody interested should get in touch with his local area office of the NCB, it said.

I tore out the advertisement and asked my editor on the *Galloway Gazette* for a week's holiday. Ten days later I was in Newcastle. I went along to the Team Valley headquarters of the Durham area of the NCB and asked to speak to the head of manpower.

"Well, Mr Fraser, you have come all the way from Stranraer, you say?"

"Yes."

"Would you like something to eat — say a sausage roll and a cup of tea?"

"No, that's all right, thanks."

"Well, obviously you are very keen and I like to see that in a young man, but really I cannot add to anything I wrote in the letter to you. We just don't have any vacancies at the moment, I am afraid."

So I produced the *Sun* cutting from my inside coat pocket and said, "Why are you advertising for people to come and work in the mines, then?"

"But that is for manual labour."

"But that is exactly what I want to do."

"Oh, I see. That's quite different. Ah, you see, we were under the impression, what with your qualifications, that you wanted to join the clerical staff here at the NCB."

"No, no. I just want to be an ordinary miner."

"Oh, well, in that case . . ."

And he sent me along to see a different head of manpower who was also amazed that I had travelled all the way from Stranraer. When I told him why I had come to see him, he shook his head and said, "I am sorry, but you are just too late. It's a pity you didn't apply to me a couple of weeks ago before we started this advertising campaign. You see the response has been amazing. We have got two thousand applicants for only a thousand vacancies here in the Durham area, and really you are not local and it is our policy always to give the locals the first option on any jobs going."

"So that means I will never be able to become a miner."

"I wouldn't say that. Why don't you try applying at your local area branch of the NCB?"

"That's the whole point. I originally come from Inverness and there aren't any coal mines there."

He pondered and eventually said, "Well, I will see what I can do for you, but I am not promising anything, mind."

A few telephone calls later I was fixed up with an interview at Westoe Colliery in South Shields. I was lucky because the Westoe personnel manager was interviewing applicants that very afternoon.

As I did not have any transport, a car was laid on for me and I was chauffeur-driven to Westoe Colliery. The chauffeur was an ex-miner who had been injured down the pit.

I was expecting a long interview. Instead the personnel manager, in between phone calls, asked my name, age and address and told me that he would write and tell me when and where to go for a medical examination.

A few weeks later a letter instructed me to go to Whitburn Colliery. It meant travelling right across Scotland on three trains and a bus. I remember it was raining as I arrived at the medical centre. The door was locked and I knocked.

"Yes, what do you want?"

"I've come for my medical examination."

"What's wrong with you?"

"There's nothing wrong with me."

"Well, what are you doing here then?"

"I tell you, I have come for my medical examination. I need to pass it before I can start work down the pit."

"What?"

"I said I have —"

"I heard you, pal, but we're not holding medical examinations today."

"But you must be. It says so here."

And I showed him my letter. It transpired that I had gone to the wrong Whitburn. The medical examinations were being held at Whitburn Colliery, Tyne and Wear, not Whitburn Colliery, Lothian.

So I rang up the personnel manager at Westoe. He wasn't the least bit sympathetic. "Well, you have had your chance and I am afraid you have blown it." But he eventually relented and he organized for me to go for a medical examination at Killock Colliery in Cumnock.

My eyes were tested and my lungs X-rayed. The doctor

asked me if I had any diseases and looked at my hands and prodded my chest. I did not pull in my stomach and try to look muscular. Far better for the doctor to declare me inadequate for pit work than for me to be ignominiously sacked after a couple of weeks.

I passed my medical and was informed that I was to start on 2 September 1977. I finished with my newspaper at the end of July and that left me with the month of August in which to do something constructive about my body. I planned a daily routine of forty press-ups first thing in the morning and last thing at night, a three-mile run and half an hour's digging in the garden. I actually managed about half of that and by the end of the holiday I felt fit if not strong. I also regularly washed my hands in paraffin which is supposed to harden your skin but by the time I reached South Shields my hands were still far from being the tough knotty fists of a manual labourer.

Letter 1

Dear Teddy,

You can expect letters from me whenever anything happens or, I suppose, whenever I feel inclined. The point is that you won't be receiving them regularly. You will get them at the important times, maybe four times one month and not at all the next.

Well, here goes . . . I have been here for four days and they are like the first days at a new school. All the other boys are much bigger than me and they all seem to have masses to say to one another. The only comfort I get is the end of the day when I climb into bed and burrow into my blankets. Bed is delicious because it's all mine. For the while it takes me to drop off to sleep I can enjoy shutting out all the rough incomprehensible noise of the outside world. Mind you, if it provides the best time of my new life, it also gives me the rudest shock when I am woken by the alarm clock, which I have to pounce on so nobody else in the room is disturbed. And I am up against another long day.

Do you remember the kind of boy who had the worst time at Ampleforth? The bewildered little foreigner, fresh from France, who didn't understand a word of any schoolboy slang or much else of what was going on around him. That's how I feel here. I just can't understand what anybody is saying. I have said about forty words today and maybe twenty-eight of them were

"What?" In fact just about the only words I can make out with confidence in the Geordie dialect are the swear words, which occur as frequently as adjectives.

My digs are pretty dismal. They were advertised in the local paper, the *Shields Gazette*. They will do for the meantime until I get myself properly organized. I think it's called a working man's lodging-house, which is a joke because I am practically the only person here who has got a job. There are twelve lodgers in the house and about half of them are single men who talk about having to "do some business in town" when really they mean they have to go to the launderette or change some books at the library. For £16 a week I get one cooked meal a day, a drawer and a half for my belongings and a top bunk to sleep in. I share my bedroom, which is only marginally bigger than the kitchen, with three old men. We all have to be meticulous about undressing. Each of us has a different place in the room to put his clothes. I drape mine on that part of the settee which is nearest my bunk. My socks I keep in my shoes. It is especially important for me to know exactly where everything is because I am on the four in the morning shift which actually means getting up in the pitch dark at 3.15 a.m.

I catch the pit bus at 3.30 and arrive about half an hour later at Seaham Colliery where there is an assembly room in which eighty of us trainees from all over the Durham area congregate. On the first day we were divided into sixteen groups of five, each of which was allocated an instructor for underground training. So far we have just been in the classroom where I have been told that the earth is like a cream cake. The icing is everything that grows on top. The marzipan is the earth. The sponge represents the rock and the layer of cream in the middle of the cake is coal. So what happens is that you sink a shaft through the sponge to get to the cream, which you then extract. Now imagine the cake covers an area of one thousand square miles. Obviously it is neither practical nor efficient to bring the coal up through just one outlet. So shafts are sunk all over the cake thus explaining how it is that pits miles apart from one another can in fact be used to mine the same seams of coal.

The NCB can have no exaggerated opinion of the intelligence of their employees, being staunch believers in education through repetition. We were given a questionnaire to complete. We had to fill in the gaps. It took five pages, for example, to make one simple statement, namely: "A gas known either as firedamp or methane is released when coal is broken up." The trainee had to fill in the dashes. On page 3 it says: "When we dig for coal and break it loose from the strata the trapped — is released". Page 4: Answer — gas. "In every coalmine as the coal is broken up a certain amount of — is released." Page 5: Answer — methane gas. "As the methane gas is released from coal, it is mixed with a small amount of other gases which have also been trapped in the coal. The mixture of methane and a small amount of other gases is known as firedamp. Because firedamp is made up mostly of methane it is sometimes called by that name. Firedamp is often referred to as —." Page 6: Answer — methane. "When methane is released from the coal, it is mixed with a small amount of other gases, this mixture is known as —." Page 7: Answer — firedamp. "There is a small amount of other gases in firedamp. The firedamp consists mainly of —." Page 8: Answer — methane. And so on.

Our instructors can't get enough of talking about gas but I understand why they so thoroughly drill us on it. Gas explosions kill as many miners as collapsing roofs. A methane gas explosion can give off carbon monoxide and as little as 0.04% of this in the air will kill you in five minutes, they tell us. So everybody down the pit is equipped with a self-rescuer — a tin box you wear on your belt containing enough carbon monoxide antidote to keep you going for an hour.

Yours, Kit

Letter 2

Dear Teddy,

Since my last letter I have been discovered. In fact I would say that I am probably the best known of all the eighty trainees here. Word has got around that great sport is to be had at my expense because I am different. It's always the same, isn't it? Whenever you get two or three males gathered together in the name of anything one of them gets it in the neck so that the other two can feel good. In my group a wag called Stan the Man is at present milking me for laughs. This is particularly encouraged by a beer-bellied character called Bob Thomas. The other two lads in the group are quite peripheral but generally contribute insults on cue. It has now spread to other groups so anyone can take a pot shot at me.

I am not sure I don't prefer it to being completely ignored. After all, loneliness is as much a torment as victimization. At least there is contact and something to which I can react. The next step is to neutralize the hostility — even make a friend! But I am dreadfully handicapped by not being able immediately to understand what they are saying.

Actually, right now, I feel tired of it all. So I will just give you the details and you can decide for yourself how I should react. Oh, by the way, we are being trained down the pit now and that means the classes of twenty or so have been returned to our original groups of five, as read out at the first assembly. I could escape notice in a classroom but, as from the beginning of the second week, I have been at the mercy of the four fellow trainees in my group. Stan the Man never tires of throwing stones at me. He also likes to kick dust over me while I am eating my "bait" — the miners' term for snack — and stealing the helmet off my head and playing football with it — the helmet, I mean. I have had my working jacket ripped to pieces — I was wearing it at the time. Similarly, the buttons on my shirt I wear get torn off. I have had my bait stolen from my haversack and this riles me the most. There is nothing to look forward to more than your bait. Another time I found the inside of my ham sandwiches doctored with snuff. I have been sprayed with water from a drinking bottle down the pit and I have been flicked with towels in the shower.

Riding up the cage is a great opportunity for my persecutors because there is no way I can escape. There is a lad who finds it amusing to give me love bites on the neck. One of the more innocuous things they do to me in the cage is repeatedly tug my cap-lamp lead. This makes my head suddenly jerk up.

The instructors insist that we ride in the cage with our cap-lamps turned off so that nobody is dazzled. So it was totally dark yesterday when everybody in the cage started to poke my face with their forefingers. I tried to ward them off by waving my arms over my face but, of course, they got through. It was lucky my eye didn't get poked. This was at the end of the shift and when we got up on bank the next shift was waiting to go down; as we got out of the cage they all started pointing and laughing at me. I couldn't understand it. They didn't even know me. Why were they laughing at me? I didn't hang about to ask. I just made quickly for the lamp-room but on the way I passed a mirror and I caught a fleeting glimpse of my face. I went back and had a closer look. It was covered in blue felt-tip pen ink. Some of the lads had obviously not been jabbing me with fingers.

My general policy is to look as cheerful as possible and try as hard as I can to develop exchanges into conversations, especially when there are just two of us, but sometimes when I offer a little bit in what appears to be a general conversation, I get this sort of treatment: "Who's talking to you?" "Well, nobody in particular but I thought that . . ." "Well, shut your hole then."

Other times I get tricked into a rejection, for example I have been asked, "Hey, Chris, do you want a tab?" (a cigarette). "Yes." "Well, buy your own and stop scrounging all the time!"

Yesterday was payday and Bob Thomas invited me to come and have a drink with him and a couple of others from work. Bob is sometimes nice to me or, at least, every so often he shows an interest in me. So anyway I accepted. When we got to the pub, I offered to buy the first round of drinks — four pints costing about a pound. They accepted the offer. Then one of the lads asked me whether I had a girlfriend in South Shields yet. No, I hadn't.

"You want to get yerself a lass, Chris mun," he said. "Are you not a member of any nightclub yet?"

"No, I'm not."

"I tell you what. I'll get you fixed up at Rupert's. Some of the smartest fanny in the town goes there."

"That's kind of you."

"You'll need a sponsor, mind," he said, stroking his chin as if in thought. "I'll be your sponsor but that means if you cause any trouble at the club I'll get kicked out as well as you and it also means I have to fork up a pound."

"I would be grateful."

"Tell you what, Chris lad. I'll be seeing the manager tonight. I'll pay him the pound and get it all fixed up."

"Here, take this pound."

"No, no. I wouldn't hear of it, mate. Just get in the next round of drinks."

So I did. When it was time to buy the third round, two of the lads left — one excusing himself by saying he was feeling ill and the second saying he had to be away to see his lass. The third lad got up from his seat and said simply "I think it's time I was away as well. You don't want a drink, do you, Chris?"

It was one of those rhetorical questions, because he did not wait for an answer. I have since discovered that you do not need a sponsor to join Rupert's.

But that's enough of my troubles. I suppose you want to hear what it is like down a pit now that I have finally managed to get down one. Well, before I start I must warn you that Seaham is just for trainees so no coal is being excavated. It consists merely of a series of tunnels along which run trams that we are taught how

8

to clip and unclip on to haulage ropes. We also learn about bell signals to get the trams moving "inbye" and "outbye". "Inbye" means towards the coalface and "outbye" towards the shaft.

We are also taught about ventilation, which disperses any of the dreaded gases that might otherwise collect. If you leave doors open the current of air being blasted through the pit is diverted. So the big thing is to shut the ventilation door behind you whenever you go through one (cf. farmers' obsession about shutting gates).

In fact I get the impression that mining is like underground harvesting, with the light blocked out so that there are no seasons. Except of course this pit is just a shell. All the goodness has been taken out of it. Instead it has us eighty trainees rattling about inside it, permanently bashing our heads against the girders overhead. I tell you, I would be battered senseless if I didn't wear a helmet.

If Seaham is anything to go by, I think I am quite suited to coalmines. I don't get at all claustrophobic, not that there is much cause for it, considering most of the tunnels are slightly above head height. Indeed all these rounded tunnels which slope off into alcoves of work areas make me feel very cosy. It's like being in an enormous bed with a mountain of blankets on top and enough room in between the sheets to walk around in. If it weren't for the other people here I think I would be having a marvellous time.

The cage, by the way, is not at all frightening. It is no more alarming than a hotel lift but it is more fun because you feel yourself descending into the bowels of the earth. Bob Thomas tells me, however, that the cage is much bigger and faster at Westoe which is where we are both due to be employed at the end of this month's training.

Yours, Kit

Letter 3

Dear Teddy,

Thank you very much for your advice but I'm not quite sure whether it is really appropriate. I mean, let's face it, the wisdom of P. G. Wodehouse might apply for the rarefied world of the country-house party but it's meaningless down here. "Cultivating a lofty contempt" might have been just the thing to stiffen the resolve of Guss Fink Nottle before having to deliver a speech for prizegiving at a prep school but it is hardly going to make me any friends here. And that is what I want. A couple of friends. Or just one would do.

As it happens my unpopularity has plummeted to unfathomed depths due to a thoughtless mistake on my part. Yesterday all of us eighty trainees were gathered together in the assembly hall to hear the chief instructor ask if anyone wanted to change from the 4 a.m. to the 9 a.m. shift. Immediately I put up my hand. I thought it was a golden opportunity to get away from my tormentors. Maybe I would be put in with a nicer group. And anyway I can't stand having to get up at three in the morning. The chief instructor asked for my name and those of the rest of my group. He said that as from Monday my group of Stan the Man, Bob Thomas, Andy Newton, Peter Pino and myself would work the nine in the morning shift.

They were all furious with me. It means we lose our

unsocial hours allowance which amounts to £4 a week each. Peter Pino and Bob Thomas are particularly angry. Both of them have wives and families to support. At last they have all got a real reason to dislike me. After the assembly I had my jersey snatched off me and thrown out of the window of the pit bus on the way back from Seaham. By the time I had attracted the driver's attention and the bus had stopped, we were a good four hundred yards away from the place where it had been thrown. The driver said he was not prepared to wait ten minutes for me to fetch it. So I had to hitch a lift back to South Shields. Frankly I dread going back to work on Monday.

I do feel drained. I put every ounce of effort into coping so I've got nothing in reserve. It is incredible how quickly one's confidence can be eroded. I mean I am twenty-three and yet right now I don't feel a day over thirteen. It is as if the intervening ten years' work I have spent developing myself never happened. I am a "nothing" at the moment. It's as if my brain has solidified. Interestingly enough, it's not misery I feel but a sort of dullness. If I ever say anything to my mates I usually have to think before I speak.

The problem is that the only response I get is negative. I haven't had what you would call a conversation with anyone since I've been here, but it has not been for any lack of trying. Amidst all this noise of people talking and laughing and shouting, I am isolated in a cocoon of silence.

I am also proving to be pretty useless at pit work. This week we have been erecting and taking down steel girders for tunnels. I always seem to be standing around watching other members of the group doing the work. And even when I do get around to having a go, it is all I can do to keep the girder upright, let alone properly positioned so that it can be bolted to another. As far as I can see, the moment you try and do something with an unwieldy inanimate object it becomes organic. Steel girders, for example, act as if they are drunk, and you have to do all you can to stop them falling over.

We have also been taught how to erect the old-fashioned wooden pit prop and its modern counterpart — the hydraulic prop — both of which need a piece of wood placing between the lid of the prop and the roof so as to tighten the fit. The proper name for this piece of wood is "cap". Erecting the hydraulic prop is a simple job: you just work the lever up and down and the prop grows taller. When there are only a few inches to spare between its lid and the roof you slip in the cap and lever again to tighten the fit.

However, putting the old wooden pit prop up involves a lot of hard graft with a mell (a huge hammer). Really it's a two-man job. One man holds the prop and the cap in position at an off-centre angle against the roof. The other man hammers at the top of the prop and the cap repeatedly as hard as he can until he gets a ninety-degree angle formed between the line of the roof and the stance of the prop.

From the old days the cap was nicknamed a "deputy head" because you had to hit it hard with a mell to get it in place. The most effective way of summoning up the stamina and strength to keep on hammering it was to imagine it was the head of a deputy. In all this I am delegated the role of gofer: that is I go for whatever is needed for the person who is doing the hitting.

Yours, Kit

Letter 4

Dear Teddy,

Whatever I do seems to land me deeper in trouble, although it doesn't matter so much now because we have finished our training at Seaham and next Monday I start at Westoe. Anyway it has been an eventful week with my stock sinking to an all-time low.

I decided to make up the money my fellow group members lost because of my foolish application for a change of shift. From the financial point of view it doesn't bother me at all. It cost me £16 but I am not here to make any money — I am here for the experience which, so far, I am getting by the ladleful. However, as expected, I have been soundly criticized for my generosity. I have been approached by other miners who told me I was soft to make up my mates' money. They say I haven't done anything wrong in volunteering for a change in shift. If the other lads in my group had lost money by me, that was their lookout.

On reflection I think there might have been a slight swing of opinion in my favour. Some lads, including Bob Thomas, who in my view is just completely mischievous, have told me to clock Stan the Man. I have been told that that is the only way to get him off my back. I reply with great dignity, or at least that is what I am trying to reply with, that I refuse to sink to Stan's level. They say I am soft. They all talk about the necessity to be hard, which is not my style at all.

Having handed out the money which they all accepted as if it was their due, the saga took another twist. We were working up on bank, generally tidying the place up when somebody came to me and asked me if I was Chris Fraser. The pit manager wanted to see me. I was to go to his office.

"Sit down, bonny lad," the manager said, looking at me with some interest. "Now I suggest you tell me what's been going on."

"What do you mean?"

"Well, for a start, what's all this I hear about you paying other people money because they don't want to work with you on the nine in the morning shift?"

I looked as if I was going to shrug my shoulders but instead I cleared my throat, rearranged myself on my seat and said nothing.

"I haven't got all day," he said.

"I suppose it's true," I eventually replied.

"Whose idea was it?"

"Mine."

"Are you sure that nobody tried to persuade you to give them money? Because if I find out that anybody tried to get money out of you over this incident, I shall have him sacked immediately. We don't want that kind of person down the pit."

"I can assure you that nobody asked me for the money. I offered it."

"You can tell the four people concerned that if they

do not return the money before the end of the week they will be sacked."

"Right-oh," I sighed.

The manager allowed another silence to settle and I was about to get up and leave when he said in a much gentler voice than he had been using, "Are you happy here, Chris?"

"Yes, I'm all right."

"It's just that I've been hearing things."

"Oh."

"Yes. I wonder if you wouldn't be happier in a different shift altogether."

"No, no. I'm happy. I'm very happy . . . er . . ."

"But you had your face painted blue in the cage."

"Yes, that's true."

"And a couple of days ago you had to walk almost all the way back to South Shields because somebody had thrown your jersey out of the back window of the bus."

"No, I got a lift actually."

"And just yesterday you were seen walking from the assembly hall to the bus with your coat pockets on fire."

I have forgotten to mention that the lads think it is fun to lob lighted cigarettes into my coat pockets. Once or twice I did not notice until the pockets were on fire.

"It's only that I'm different," I said. "They'll get used to me."

I still haven't got a penny back from any of them. But I don't care. I'm just glad to be finished with Seaham. Let's hope Westoe is better. Mind you, Bob Thomas told me, "If you think it's rough at Seaham, just wait till you get to Westoe — they piss on you in the cage."

I think I've got through to Bob Thomas. He doesn't dislike me and I have a feeling he respects my consistency. I have survived a month of relentless persecution without losing my temper or breaking down in any other way. There is a horrible little chap at Seaham whom they call the Ferret and he once said to me, "I don't know how you put up with all this teasing."

Bob Thomas overheard the remark. He turned on the Ferret and said, "You should know, because if Chris weren't here we would be taking the piss out of you."

Yours, Kit

Letter 5

Dear Teddy,

I haven't written to you for a few weeks because up until last week nothing much happened. The only thing of note was a visit to Rupert's nightclub. It was organized by Bob Thomas for about half a dozen of the Westoe lads who had been at Seaham. I was included in this group and so was Stan the Man who, I think, is beginning to tolerate me. Of course it was Saturday night and we were all togged up in our best gear, nicely primed to slay any young hind that might happen to stray our way. If, in the hierarchy of things, Bob Thomas represented the senior stag, then with my lack of experience in these affairs I felt like a young knobber, a peripheral deer who keeps lookout for the herd.

The first part of the evening was spent visiting our various stomping grounds which, translated into common parlance, means that we went on a pub crawl. In one of the pubs we came across a couple of lasses sipping vodkas together. Bob Thomas invited them to an orgy but they laughed him off by saying that an orgy sounded a bit tame for them. After a while they collected their handbags and left.

I find pub crawls very unsatisfactory. It leads to a disjointed evening. You can't settle in any pub, not that you would want to in South Shields on a Saturday night. The whole business is such a struggle — to get to the bar, to catch the barman's eye. Then there is all the kerfuffle of handing the pints in a chain over people's heads, trying to hear what people are saying, getting out of other people's way, not being able to put your pint down anywhere. Not my idea of fun.

Two things happened in the disco. I produced a press card I had kept from my days with the *Galloway Gazette* and showed it to the lads. Within a trice it was smuggled from sight and I never got it back. The other thing to happen, or not to happen as the case might have been, was that Stan disappeared for twenty minutes and when he came back he informed us that he had just scored. He said he had had a lass outside up against a wall. I had noticed that he had been dancing with a blonde just before he disappeared but where was she now? Surely she should be purring by his side and looking up at him with soft doe eyes? But as you know I am innocent in such matters.

So that deals with the nightclub visit. I don't want you to miss out on anything interesting even if it is not all that momentous. That is why I have delayed the big news until this late stage in the letter. After two weeks piffling around on bank, we have finally started our underground training at Westoe, and how different it is from Seaham!

Westoe is a big black monster with conveyor belts for arteries and coal for blood. Apart from a few manset landings which are lit up, Westoe lives in the dark. You have only the light of your cap-lamp to see where you are going. There is also the constant racket of conveyor belts rattling over their rollers which, if you are standing near them, means you have to shout to make yourself heard.

I work with a lad called Stanley under the supervision of our instructor, Ned Hawke. We spend the shift clearing slurry from under the conveyor belts and freeing rollers that are stuck fast. Ned has taken to calling me Tolstoy. He is staggered to hear that I have A-levels and he defers to me on points of information about current affairs. On the other hand he can't believe that "with all your qualifications" I appear to be so inept at anything that requires a modicum of common sense, like knowing how to shovel.

When I began I would shovel from the top of the slurry. It was Ned who taught me first to make a clearing at the base of the mound and shovel from there. Because the conveyor belts make such a din we all talk at bait stop when we sneak off into a quiet secluded corner of the pit, away also from cold ventilation current that blows inbye up to the coalface. I think I am getting on quite well with Ned and Stanley. Neither of them knows anything about my time at Seaham. Thankfully Stanley had not been in my shift, so I feel I have been given a second chance.

Ned is lenient with us. He lets us knock off from work early so that we can get grid position in the manset, the underground train. The secret is to bag a seat on the right-hand side of one of the carriages at the loco end of the manset, so that you make sure of getting a place in the first cage up. When the manset slows down to a halt at the shaft, people start jumping out of the carriages and racing for the cage where onsetters stand and count fifty people into each of three decks. It is like a game of oranges and lemons. You have raced to get a good place in the queue and you are shuffling towards the cage. You desperately hope to slip in before the arm of the onsetter comes down. If you are on the wrong side of that arm, you have to wait an extra five minutes for the second cage. Nobody has pissed on me in the cage yet and quite frankly, the first cage is so full, I doubt if there is enough room for anybody to pull it out, never mind aim it in a particular direction.

Going up at the end of the shift is joy. You've done your day's work and you have a hot shower to look forward to. But I am envious of those lucky miners who have got nice, warm wives waiting for them at home and a good solid meal bubbling away in the oven.

The cage down is an entirely different affair. Many prefer to take the second cage and the repartee, when it occurs, is halfhearted. Down we go and there's a half-hour journey in the manset to the landing where we disperse to our various places of work. Once again the journey into the mine is a more sober affair than the one out. You sit three to a bench, your knees interlocked with the three people perched opposite you. The manset trundles along at a speed that is not supposed to exceed 10 m.p.h., though it feels a lot faster. And so for half an hour we rattle along till we reach the landing. By this time we are over four miles out into the North Sea. I tell you it is an odd sensation knowing there are five hundred feet of ocean above you.

Yours, Kit

Letter 6

Dear Teddy,

I have changed digs and at last I have got a room of my own with a nice juicy double bed in it. So if I do manage to get myself a girl at least I have got somewhere to take her back, lay her down and do the dirty deed of darkness. But, as yet, my only bedmate is my pillow.

In actual fact I am not very lonely. My shift down the pit occupies my day and it tires me so much that, when I get to my digs, I am quite happy just to pick up a book, watch a bit of telly or go and have a couple of solitary pints.

My one visitor is my landlord, Frank, who makes my evening meal and breakfast for me. From what I can gather his wife owns and runs everything. The advantage of his position is that he does nothing all day except the occasional chore — like cooking for me. Once in the morning and once in the evening — he is utterly punctual — he drives from his wife's first house, where they live, to his wife's second house, where I now nestle as a solitary lodger.

Apart from my bedroom on the ground floor and the sitting-room upstairs the house is locked up. Frank even locks the kitchen once he has washed up after I have finished my meal, which consists of regulation doses of meat, veg and tatties, courtesy of Messieurs Heinz and Findus — all eminently digestible after a long day down the pit. This is usually followed by a pudding like apple crumble liberally sprinkled with hundreds and thousands. Then I sit down in the armchair with a cigarette. When he has finished washing up he joins me in the sitting-room and, lighting up his pipe, spends ten minutes either being snide or self-pitying. If he is being snide I reply as cheerfully and as innocently as I can, pretending not to notice his sarcasm and, I think, sometimes that aggravates him.

Frank is highly suspicious, which has got something to do with my being the only tenant in the house. He reckons that anybody who is reduced to putting up with rented accommodation for any length of time must be an unsavoury sort of character. Anybody respectable would have established himself somewhere in a house of his own. Anyway, he is mighty prone to evicting his tenants and he tells me with relish of the disreputable people he has had to get rid of in the past.

One thing's for sure. He is absolutely perplexed by me. He can't understand what on earth a "well-spoken" lad like me is doing working down the pit and is determined to find out. I am sure he thinks I am hiding from a disgusting past and is just waiting for the moment it catches up with me. Out of curiosity he won't evict me until he has discovered my foul misdeed.

When Frank has finished his pipe, he sprays the air with an aerosol can of air-freshener. Sometimes he sprays the room when he first comes in so while he's cooking I open all the windows in the hope of dispersing the soapy atmosphere by the time supper arrives.

I am getting on well with Stanley and Ned. They love hearing about my trials and tribulations with my landlord. Stanley and I spend a lot of time grinning, probably because we share frustrations like rollers which refuse to roll and mounds of slurry that don't seem to diminish in size no matter how hard we dig.

We have also been making water channels. Some parts of the pit are wet — indeed most pitmen here wear wellies. Huge puddles, formed by water dripping from the roof, have to be drained away. So Stanley and I are set to work by Ned digging one-foot-deep channels. We do this with a pickaxe and a shovel. Occasionally we have to navigate our channels through tram tracks by means of little dams.

The other job we are called on to do is stonedusting. The point of stonedust is that it prevents an explosion ricocheting up a tunnel. Also it makes the pit look nice. Stonedust is white powder. We cut open a hundredweight sack of the stuff and spread it around with our spades like it was fertilizer in a garden. It makes it look as if snow has fallen in the pit. Apparently, if somebody important comes to visit, stonedusting is a priority. Prince Philip probably thinks coalmines are white.

Stanley and I have taken to teasing Ned about his habit of harking back to the old times when, according to him, you had to have coalmining in your blood if you were to survive down the pit.

"Oh aye," he says. "There were not many Bevan boys who stayed once the war had stopped. But now it's different, you get all sorts coming down here — bloody ex-bus conductors, butchers, bakers and even a bastard college boy." That last, of course, was for my benefit. "Bringing machines down the pit never did any good. It has made active men lazy and lazy men lazier still. Oh aye, we were more content in the old days when you had to work hard."

"Used to work in a eight-inch seam with five inches of water, didn't you Ned? And those were the days before snorkels and flippers."

"Ah, you can laugh but you don't know how lucky you are."

"I thought you just said we were unlucky because we have machines which make us lazy."

"I tell you who's unlucky, bonny lad, and that's me having to spoonfeed you two slackers through your month's training. I don't know how I am supposed to make pitmen out of you. Neither of you are fit to work in a fucking sweetshop, let alone down the pit."

I very much play second fiddle to Stanley. He is a bit of a likely lad. Good-looking with an earring, regular features, well brushed teeth which, of course, you notice down the pit, and a thriving sex life which makes him and others laugh a lot. Stanley regales us with stories of his various conquests. His latest *histoire*, which he told to a group of miners in the manset, actually shocked me. He had agreed to meet his girlfriend after the pub shut to take her off to a nightclub. But by closing time he was worse off for drink. When he met his girlfriend at the agreed place he told her that he was feeling too drunk to go to a nightclub, so why not go back to his place where they could drink coffee and listen to some records? His girlfriend lost her temper and said that that was typical. She had had enough of him. She was not in the habit of dressing up to drink cups of coffee. She would go to the nightclub by herself. Whack! Whack! "Not with a face like that you're not!" roared Stanley, massaging his fists. The story was greeted with gales of laughter by the people sitting either side of us in the manset.

Yours, Kit

Letter 7

Dear Teddy,

I am now a fully-fledged coalminer. I have been so for a couple of weeks. And do you know what I do all day? I press a button about ten times a shift, or if it is a real "rough un" I may be called to press it up to twenty times. But don't think I have been singled out for this arduous task. All the trainees from Westoe who went to Seaham with me are now on conveyor-belt buttons. And we have all got our different ways of coping with the tedium of six hours doing nothing all by yourself. (Boy, do you learn patience! I can happily wait in a bus queue for hours now with perfect equanimity.)

My one real bit of fun in the shift is turning off my cap-lamp, drinking in the darkness and imagining I am alone and lost a thousand feet under the sea. After a while I begin to panic a little. It may sound silly but the adrenalin rush helps relieve the tedium. Sadly, the feeling soon goes and you can't repeat it too often. So I now do it just once a shift.

Otherwise I fall into a light sleep whenever I possibly can, clean up slurry with a shovel, eat some bait, read, go tightrope walking on the tram rails, talk to myself, have some more bait, read and finally walk up and down a thirty-yard stretch.

My nearest neighbour is an Irish lad called Paddy who is about a hundred yards away on the Second Sutcliffe button — the draughtiest and coldest button position in our district. Paddy is a great walker. He likes to walk, so he says, two miles before bait and two miles after bait without straying further than the requisite thirty yards from his button. Slack Mack, who is kept at the TB80 button, which is horribly noisy because it is situated near an air booster, enjoys shouting and screaming whenever the mood takes him. Don Pyle just ploughs through crossword puzzles. Others read porn.

By every button is a "dac" which is a pit intercom. It has three buttons: one to speak, a second which nobody really uses much and a third which lets out a shrill beep-like noise. This beeper is invaluable for waking up fellow button lads and warning them of the imminent arrival of an undermanager or a colliery overman. I have an arrangement with Paddy, my neighbouring button lad, that if either of us gives ten beeps the other will know there is a high official in the vicinity. You can always tell an official way off in the dark of a tunnel by his two lights — his cap-lamp and his safety-lamp. If only one light is approaching you can relax.

Yours, Kit

Letter 8

Dear Teddy,

I have been promoted to the stageloader button at F55 coalface. Colliery overman, Jim Casey, apparently thinks that the talents of a lad of my education should not be wasted on an ordinary button. Really I never knew my A-levels were going to come in so useful! They have got me to within five yards of the coalface.

I will tell you all about what my new job entails in my next letter. This letter I want to devote to giving you my first impressions of the coalface. It is not a disappointment. And that is saying something considering how much I have looked forward to this moment.

Imagine me sitting under one of the hundred and ninety one-ton steel chocks that stand in a row along the two-hundred-yard-long, six-foot-high gleaming black coalface of F55. In front of me is a rippling black stream of coal travelling along the metal panzer belt to the stageloader and the first conveyor belt outbye. I hear the noise getting louder and louder and the dust is getting thicker. We are at the mulligate end of the coalface and there are half a dozen other men crouched under various chocks, waiting for the arrival of the shearer, or the machine as it is also called. The monster is coming and it's being led by Eddie Robson.

Here it is! Tons of steel, a ball of mechanical fury,

spinning a revolving disc studded with evil picks, tearing coal off the face and spewing it on to the panzer. As it motors past us on its journey up the wall, the mulligate chockmen advance the chocks forward and timber up the gouged face. Later, from behind us comes the sound of the outrage of Mother Earth. The roof falls in behind us to form the goaf. That's the most powerful thing I've ever heard. It's got more resonance than a bomb. Do you remember the one we heard go off at Cromwell Road Air Terminal?

The goaf is the area filled in behind the chocks after they have advanced. Sometimes the goaf is not formed for two or three shears but when the roof finally falls it sounds like the earth's tummy rumbling, only you are right in beside it.

I must just tell you about chocks. Powered by hydraulics, their two metal arms go slowly up and down according to whether you push or pull a lever. They are like decapitated, stationary sleepwalkers with clown shoes on. Imagine 190 of them standing in a row facing a wall. To get from one end to the other of the wall, you have to crawl along in between the outstretched arms and the clown shoes. That's how the men make their way along the face, clambering over the chocks' feet like overweight monkeys and ducking under their arms.

The purpose of the chock is to hold up the roof, just like the pit props of yesteryear. Its arms stretch out over the panzer and the shearer, thus providing cover for the machine man. Timber, in the form of inchboards and chock knobs, is fitted in between the arms of a chock and the roof above it. Once it has been "timbered up", the chockman pulls his lever and the arms rise, pushing the timber right up against the roof so that the latter has no space in which to fall.

In the old days the men had the laborious task of taking pit props and putting them up and taking the face belt to bits and reassembling it every time the wall moved forward. Nowadays both operations are done merely by pulling and pushing chock levers.

How dangerous is it at the coalface? Well, as yet, it is too early to answer that for definite as I have been here only a couple of weeks, but I would still like to give an opinion, even if I might have to retract it at a later date. I desperately want to tell you because I think it is all so surprising.

From what I have seen so far at F55 face and heard from the men there, in actual fact a coalface is one of the safest places in the pit. Furthermore the work, for the most part, is not very physically demanding. The two main sources of danger in the pit are falling roofs and runaway trams. Obviously there are no trams on the coalface and also there is no better protection in the pit against a fall of roof than a chock. As long as you obey safety regulations and keep under a chock while you are at the face, you are perfectly safe.

What air-raid shelters are to dropping bombs, chocks are to falling roofs. You are virtually crush-proof. An occasional little tumble of rubble can slip in through the gaps in the woodwork and between the chocks, but boulders do not get through and it is the boulders that break bones. Admittedly machine men and anybody else who steps over to the coalface side of the panzer run the risk of injury should they stand beyond the chocks. This they might do when changing the picks on the disc of the shearer or just timbering up. There will always be an area of naked roof in between the end of a chock arm and the face.

How hard is coalface work? So far I haven't seen anybody do anything that I couldn't do. In fact people seem to spend a lot of the shift doing nothing, just waiting for the shearer to come their way or for some piece of machinery to be mended. I would say the average shift of a faceman could easily be done by a housewife. His job is simply after each shear to pull a hydraulic lever which rams over some ordinary-sized chocks at the wall, and two king-sized chocks at the junction of the mulligate tunnel. The two fitters, chock-maintenance man and electrician do not stir from their transformer until something has gone wrong and needs to be mended. Neither the face overman nor the deputy is required to break sweat while performing his task of supervision. The only miners on the face who need to deploy any effort are the two machine men. But even they require only the stamina of a man who mows his lawn. Up and down the face they walk with their respective machines — a tiring exercise sometimes because it is airless and the face lies on a slight incline. At least the machine men sweat a bit, which is more than I can say for the mulligate chockmen.

Yours, Kit

PS: Don Pyle, the lad I am replacing on the stageloader

button and who is training me at the moment, has introduced me to a card school on the manset. As we rattle along through the tunnels we play a game called switch which is a variation of whist. The best player is Paddy who used to be on the neighbouring button.

Letter 9

Dear Teddy,

I am now in full operational control of the stageloader button.

Basically the stageloader button lad is responsible for communication to and from the coalface. Any official from either up on bank or outbye, who wants to talk to anybody working on F55 coalface will in future have to do it through me. I have a black telephone that connects me with Control on bank, a district dac for anybody outbye and the face tannoy which puts me in contact with the men on the coalface. Control likes to be kept informed and the black phone gives five rings and I pick it up and say, "F55 Stageloader here."

"It's Control. Where's the machine?"

"Hold on a sec and I'll find out." Now I walk over to face tannoy and ask, "Could somebody tell me where the machine is?"

"It's on the wall."

"What?"

"It's at sixty chock going towards the tailgate."

Now you might think the job's easy but it's not. You see, the stageloader is situated downwind of the machine so it means that the air is a fog of fine debris. Whenever I take off my mask to answer a phone or a tannoy, I am taking in mouthfuls of coal and stone dust. I can feel it even now. When I am lying in bed thinking about the dust, I imagine it forming drifts in my nose and in my ears. If I sit up suddenly I can feel the back of my throat filling up like an egg-timer.

The next thing is the stageloader itself which is a huge metal machine that connects the face panzer to the first belt outbye. It makes a hell of a din. In fact I reckon I must be in the noisiest and dustiest place in the pit. It certainly means I can hardly hear a damn thing. The Geordie dialect is difficult enough for me to understand at the best of times but when it is transmitted over a dac or a telephone and I've got the stageloader rattling away beside me, it is all I can do to pick out any of the words.

I am approaching the thing as if it is a new language and I try to fasten onto key words that most frequently crop up. So now if I hear the word, "Vzarym" I know it translates as "What's the time?" "Vyzammara wi ya sheen, mun?" is "What's the matter with the machine, man?" If I can distinguish the word "water", I just go to the tap on the water pipe that is used to dampen down the dust at the machine and turn the tap on if it is off and off if it is on. If I reckon I have heard the word "electrician", I go and find one and tell him he is wanted on the face tannoy — similarly with the words that sound as if they could be "fitter", "deputy" or "overman". One sound I never fail to respond to is "stayowah" which is my name, "stageloader". When I hear that, my ears perk up like a pet dog and I jump to my feet and answer, usually with the words, "What did you say?" or "Can you repeat that?"

My biggest blunder so far happened the day before

yesterday when I was told over the face tannoy to see if the deputy was in the mulligate. Then the voice jabbered on about what I should tell the deputy once I had found him. However I could not understand exactly what the voice wanted me to tell the deputy. So after a couple of "What?"s I just said "Right-oh" and went in search of the deputy. He was not far away mending part of the TB80 belt. He looked up at me and said, "Can't you see I'm busy? Find out what I am wanted for." So I had to go back to the tannoy and ask the voice why he needed the deputy. The voice spoke as slowly and as clearly as it could and I thought I could make out the words, "Tell Geordie to get a bandit from the cage."

Such a request did not sound so very unusual to me because I have heard enough pit jargon to know that anything is possible. After all, if there is such a thing as a "bull" (an abnormally large girder used to stop runaway trams), a "hedgehog" (a tangle in a haulage rope) and a "dog" (a type of nail used by waylayers to tack rails on to their sleepers); why not a "bandit"? I imagined that perhaps a bandit was a special type of shifter and the cage was the tin box in which it was kept. Anyway I relayed the message exactly as I had heard it.

He had to go to the tannoy himself to find out what was wanted. It was not a bandit from the cage but a bandage from the first-aid canister that was needed. A man had injured himself on the coalface.

One of the good things about my present job is that I get to know the men on the face, especially those working at the mulligate end because they take their bait by my stageloader. They are all older men, except for mulligate chockman Morris Givens who is about twenty-eight, but even he's married with a couple of children. So really I am the only youngster amongst them. This is reflected in their attitude towards me. It is not that they are condescending to me, although in this environment I am obviously not their equal; it is just that it enables them to adopt something approaching an avuncular tone with me. Of course, a more unlikely bunch of uncles you never did come across — a mob of spitting, swearing, snuff-snorting black faces.

You have got to watch it with anybody who chews tobacco because there is always a chance of being hit by a glob of surplus saliva. Machineman Eddie Robson cut me off a slice to chew the other day. It makes you salivate like mad. Instead of spitting out the saliva, I swallowed it. Eddie roared with laughter. I was coughing, gasping and spluttering. Tobacco chewing is actually difficult. First you have got to learn to prevent your wad of tobacco disintegrating in your mouth. Then with your tongue pushing it against your teeth, you have to extract the juice. Next you must try and expel it without spitting the wad out as well. Besides that, it tastes horrible.

However, I don't mind the occasional pinch of snuff. You put a line of brown powder on the back of your hand, park your nostril adjacent to one end and snuff it up. Gives you a nice little lift. About twice as powerful as coffee.

John the Pole is utterly addicted to the stuff. He gets through a couple of tubes a day. He also pinches on bank, which is highly unusual because most people take snuff only as a substitute for cigarettes. Obviously smoking is forbidden down the pit. A naked flame could ignite a pocket of methane gas and we'd all go up in a puff of smoke.

The other thing about John the Pole is that he is a compulsive worker. Theoretically when they are not ramming forward or timbering up, mulligate chockmen should occupy themselves clearing up spillages of coal. In actual fact nobody bothers unless the spillage is so large that it prevents either the free run of the panzer or the chocks being rammed forward. Our mulligate end, however, is kept spotless by John the Pole. The other two chockmen spend this intervening time sitting under chocks reading newspapers, flicking through porn mags or having a quiet snooze.

The two machinemen, Eddie and Davy, are great marras — that is pit slang for mates. You never see one without the other. They work either side of the same machine. They take their bait together. The one will wait for the other to gather his things at the end of the shift and they will ride the manset sitting side by side. They will even wash each other's backs in the showers. The other day they asked me what I was doing working down the pit when I had had a decent education and what they called "qualifications". I told them that in my previous job working as a local reporter on a small weekly newspaper I had to work a sixty-hour week for £45 gross, so when one day I read in the press about coalminers getting £100 a week I decided to switch career. That made them laugh. For they knew my take-home pay is £35 a week. Surely a newspaperman should know better than to believe what he reads in the newspaper, they roared.

Yours, Kit

Letter 10

Dear Teddy,

I am beginning to be noticed in my shift at Westoe and not at all unfavourably. I will try to explain how I think this has come about.

Over the last month since I've come out of training, I have had to fend for myself again back in the larger group. Our little company of three — Ned Hawke, Stanley and myself — has been broken up and we've had to go our own separate ways into different shifts and districts. My shift consists of about 150 people of whom approximately a quarter have recently (over the last five years) gained employment down the pit. The rest are older pitmen, maybe half of whom worked in the days before mechanization. It is these older pitmen who dominate our shift and there is a happier atmosphere than at Seaham.

The lads are still boisterous, but that's normal. Periodic bouts of quarrelling and slanging, liberally interspersed with rollicking good humour, make up social intercourse down the pit. The main thing, however, is that I have not reverted to being the general receptacle for everybody's ill feeling and I put that down to the buffeting influence of the older pitmen. Miners are permanently teasing one another and certain younger ones find themselves more the butt than others, but it seems never to get to the point of persecution.

Basically, these mature old veterans want a bit of a laugh without necessarily seeing somebody being made miserable.

Also, I was completely unprepared for Seaham. I was just hit by a series of events. Now I have had time to think and work out how to fit into this society. I know it is impossible for me to become a hard Geordie lad like the rest of them but at least I can make myself acceptable. Another thing I have realized is that as long as you can show some spirit and humour you will earn respect — and without respect you are sunk. You have got to be loud too. The other day one of the F55 facemen, Tommy Pearson, told me, "If you don't use your mouth down here you just get forgotten. I was a quiet little lad when I started down the pit. You wouldn't have recognized me. Look at me now. I am the biggest loud mouth on the face and I have the most fun."

So I have taken to projecting myself — a sort of caricature of a toff. I have come out of the defensive position I adopted at Seaham and am trying to become loud and flamboyantly different and, you know, this ridiculous policy seems to be paying off. Don't you think it is ironic that to fit in to this alien society I have to highlight and exaggerate the differences between myself and the people I want to get on with?

Another thing is that though they are, almost to a man, good solid Labour voters, they actually hold some unbelievably right-wing opinions. You often hear miners saying that if anybody on the dole puts his mind to it, he can get himself a job. "Half of them are bloody scroungers." And I have heard many a pitman say that they should bring back capital punishment. So I speak up for the cause of leniency. The other day I pleaded for industrial democracy, only to be met by a hail of objections. It is marvellous if you are different and you've got something to say. You are the centre of attention and people's animosity is diverted by the subject under discussion.

Racism is rampant down here but it is all theory and very humorous. The reason for this well nigh unanimous opinion about Africans, Indians and Chinese is, I suppose, something to do with the fact that the pit is just about exclusively a white community. Up until recently jobs down the pit had been handed down from father to son and the emergence of a noticeable immigrant population has coincided with a massive shedding of labour in the country's coalmines. Anyway when Ned Hawke told me that the best thing to do with Africans was to nail them to the walls of classrooms and use them as blackboards, I pointed out that without their labour the social infrastructure of this country would collapse overnight.

"Nothing good comes of a coon", was his solemn response. "Even if you put them in a concrete mixer and turned them into tarmac and used them for the maintenance and repair of motorways, they would be no good. They wouldn't keep still, would they? You would have your M1s and M6s walking all over the fucking countryside!"

Religion is pretty well non-existent here as well. I would say the overwhelming majority of people here don't believe in God, although I have come across several agnostics. All this outright disbelief and tentative awareness prompts me, of course, to come barging in with a good, thick, solid wedge of faith. I tell them how great God is and how in the next world you get punished for not believing in Him. They are already spending most of this life underground, I say, and it looks as if they are going to spend the whole of their next life underground as well.

Sex is not such an easy subject about which to be controversial because you run the risk of sounding like a virgin and/or a homosexual. So although I have taken to saying that, by and large, I find sex a murky business, I do conform to a certain extent by boasting of mythical conquests and peering into tabloid newspapers and saying, "Cor, I would like to fuck that!"

Mind you, sometimes I am truthful, especially in the Monday-morning manset when a sort of ritualized boasting takes place about the events of the weekend.

"You should have seen me on Saturday night. I was that paralytic. I'd had ten pints. And then some bastard tried to pick a fight with me, so I just about killed him."

"I went to the Tavern and got my hole twice. Mind, it's amazing considering the condition I was in. I had had bastard fifteen pints, at least."

"I spent the whole afternoon playing pool. Never lost once."

"And Chris, what did you do?"

"Ooh, I drank nearly fourteen pints."

"What do you mean — nearly fourteen pints?"

"Well, five pints."

"But that's nowhere near bloody fourteen pints."

"No, it isn't, is it? But I almost got my hole at the Chelsea Cat."

"How's that?"

"Well, I spent about five minutes exchanging longing, lustful looks with this charming young girl. I was about to walk over to her and ask her for a dance — which would inevitably have led to a certain amount of passion on the dance floor, followed by a few drinks at the bar, followed by a sneaky invitation to come back to my place to have a look at my stamp album — when at the crucial moment her boyfriend appeared. If he had not arrived just exactly then, it would have been too late for him. Boys, oh boys! I just sweat to think how close I was to getting my hole!"

"Anything else?"

"I almost won a game of darts against Paddy on Saturday afternoon, didn't I, Paddy?"

"Aye, yer came second."

Yours, Kit

Letter 11

Dear Teddy,

At long living last I have made a friend, I think. At least I have been knocking around with him recently. Over this last week he has been on transport work and has chosen to have his bait with me. We walk to the manset together, he is one of the card school of which I am a member and on Saturday we went out to the pub and played pool together. If that doesn't add up to friendship then I don't know what does. I have saved the final proof till last. Deputy Geordie Smith came up to me at the stageloader and said, "Your *friend* Paddy has got himself transport pay this week." I mean *he* said it, not me.

Paddy, or John as he likes to be called — by his friends, is one of those nomadic Irishmen who gallivant around England picking up jobs here and there, enjoying what in later life he will probably describe as his "roving days". In his time he has earned the occasional pile of money, either from hard physical work or a lucky run on the horses, and then in a wild, drunken week or two blown his winnings sky-high. He boasts he once lived off his horses for nine months but, "It was hard work, studying form every morning. The enjoyment was going out of it. And another thing I noticed. My game was deteriorating." His game is pool. Oh there's nothing he hasn't done. He has worked on road gangs and brick sites and oil rigs and now he is trying the coalmines.

"The money's no good here but you've got security and that's a good thing to have in the winter. It can be nice and warm down here too if you know where to go."

He always knows where to go. Look at the way he has wangled this transport job. All of us button lads are waiting to be put on transport — the money is better and you are doing a proper job — but we'll probably have to wait weeks yet. Paddy, sorry I mean John, my friend, joined the pit the same time as the rest of us from Seaham.

"You can put it down to skullduggery, the sort that you learn in Donegal. That's where the clever people come from," says he with a laugh. He says everything quickly and with a laugh. He looks like Father Christmas as a young man: a red beard wrapped round a jolly face and a pair of twinkling little blue eyes. He told me that he was the original seven-stone weakling though now, aged thirty, he has got a solid steel chest with biceps to match.

"I can handle myself," he says, "and I've been up against some real hard types and seen them off the premises."

To play pool with him is an education. He overwhelms the opposition, prancing round the table, cue in one hand, pint of beer in the other, sizing up the ball with a practised eye. Then down goes the pint and up goes the cue and, barely pausing to aim, he executes a clean crisp shot and the appropriate ball is sunk in a pocket. Up comes his face in smiles.

"Now, true enough, that was a beautiful shot and a lucky one too. You see, it's the luck that puts the shine on the skill that makes it beautiful."

His self-confidence, nourished by self-applause, invariably sweeps him to another glorious victory.

I think what has drawn us together is that we are in a similar position. We are both foreigners speaking with non-Geordie accents. We are also bachelors living in digs. We both look odd: him with his red hair and beard and me with my face — well you know what it looks like, a lot of nose and not much else. We both have our idiosyncrasies. The other day he bought for his bait a loaf of bread and a tin of sardines. He gouged a hole in the middle of the loaf and poured the contents of his sardine tin into it.

John's other accomplishments are harmonica-playing, joke-telling and singing of Irish songs like "Danny Boy" and "The Wild Colonial Boy". What I admire in him is the way he gives the subject at hand — whether it be a person, a puzzle, a joke or a song — his whole beaming self. This, I think, explains his magnetism.

If the secret to a successful life is never to be at a loss for a word, then John is doing well for himself. He takes pride in being able to cap anybody else's remark. I am seeking to develop the art myself because, apart from making for witty exchanges, it is always worth keeping your end up. His example has encouraged me to adopt the comic persona of a Victorian toff. For instance I replied to Arthur Vanackter who was giving me a stream of abuse about my cloth ears. "I say, are you shouting at me? What an extraordinary person you are!"

"That's it, Chrissy lad. You tell him!" shouted one of the men over the noise of the general laughter.

My other *bon mot* was to minerman Hughie Ballon who has taken it into his head to try and shock me. He dropped his trousers and pants in front of me and squatted on a shovel as if to have a shit. By the way, there are no lavatories down the pit and if you are caught short it is thought quite acceptable to shit on your shovel and then bung the turds on the conveyor belt. This, in fact, was what had prompted Hughie to give his demonstration. He was just showing me the approved method when I dismissed him with the words, "Animals like you should be tethered to a stake."

You get the tone. It is all very snooty and not at all like me normally but it seems to go down well here. It's like a Frenchman in England is expected to overdo Gallic flattery. If we tried that sort of flannel on a girl, she'd tell us to go and take a jump, wouldn't she? Perhaps I should try it, as one thing that I have learned is that silent adoration is a waste of time. I haven't got the profile for it, and neither have you. Yes, perhaps there is a lesson to be learned here. Perhaps my experiences down the pit are teaching me things about life in general.

Anyway I'm going to have to do something to get a girl. They are beginning to notice at work and the last thing I want is for them to find out I am a virgin. Arthur Vanackter made a suspiciously acute comment the other day. I was contributing my little bit to a general conversation about sex and he turned round on me and said, "I bet if you pulled your foreskin back, moths would fly out."

The great thing about the pit is that no one can see you blushing.

Yours, Kit

PS: An interesting item for you about cap-lamps. When you want to look closely at something in the dark down the pit, you have to tilt your head so that the light from your cap lamp shines on whatever it is you are trying to see. I am now catching myself doing this on bank in broad daylight. Imagine how odd I must look in the pub straight after a shift — especially if, as often happens, my eyes are still mascara'd with coal dust — addressing myself to my pint as if I am going to pour the beer on to my forehead.

Letter 12

Dear Teddy,

We had great sport at the stageloader the other shift. Mulligate chockman Ronnie Ritchard roasted the undermanager.

Coalface production had been stopped for at least half the shift because the TB80 belt was broken. There was a rip where the belt had ridden the stageloader. About half a dozen men from the face were trying to mend it so that production could recommence. At the same time there was an argument raging about whether productivity bonus should be paid to the men during the stoppage.

The black phone rang and I answered. It was the undermanager from Control on bank. He said he wanted to speak to an official. Ronnie Ritchard took the phone because there wasn't an official present. Both the face deputy and overman were arguing with men at the tailgate of F55 face. Within minutes Ronnie was arguing with the undermanager. We all crowded round the phone and roared with laughter at Ronnie's audacity. I made a mental note at the time to remember word for word Ronnie's sallies, "Oh, come on, even our nine-year-old son knows that!" . . . "Haven't you heard that yet? I mean you have really got to do better than that!" . . . "Right, I want you to see me tomorrow morning." He did not say that he, Ronnie, wanted to see him, the undermanager. He was telling the undermanager to wait on him, the mulligate chockman. It was priceless.

There was nothing the undermanager could do, having got himself into the situation, except to put the phone down. You cannot sack anybody for insurbordination at Westoe, especially not someone like Ronnie who is the best marra of Walter Slater, the chairman of Westoe Lodge.

Our poor old undermanager! His problem is that he is young — he looks about thirty-eight — and worse still, he is a soft-spoken southerner. Anything gentle gets hammered in the pit. F55 overman Arthur Vanackter calls him "petal" and "flower" to his face. Behind his back he is accused of a lack of practical experience. They say his knowledge comes from college books and not from the coalface itself. However, to me he looks as if he knows what he is doing and frankly I think he is a nice guy.

In the mines a man is expected to stand up for himself or he is nothing. It is a fact of which I am constantly being reminded.

The other shift my district dac had broken down and on two separate occasions I was told by a deputy to go and use the TB80 dac two hundred yards away instead. I was about to walk outbye to the TB80 button for the second time when I was stopped by machineman Eddie Robson who was having his bait by the stageloader.

"You divn't wanna gang oot there, lad," he shouted.

"What?"

"You don't want to go all the way out to the TB80 button just because the deputy is too idle to go himself.

You fucking stay put, mun. Get on to the outside phone and ring up the union and tell them you are having to walk half a mile every time you want to say something over the dac. Stand up for yourself or they'll bloody walk all over you. You're as good as anybody else down the pit — deputy, overman or bastard undermanager."

As regards my personal fortunes I can say that while I have no social life at all on bank (Irish John — as people now call him — has not invited me to the pub again so I still just have the occasional pint by myself), I am making quite a name for myself down the pit.

Take today, for example. I was supposed to work the four in the morning shift but I overslept and had to work the nine in the morning instead. This meant I was working in a shift where I would not know anybody but I feel I can look after myself now. Judge for yourself. I'll give you the conversation of the manset journey inbye this morning.

I climbed in among five unknowns. They were all older pitmen and, as it turned out, one was a cockney. I had to clamber over the nearside man to get into the centre and as I stretched my leg into the middle of the compartment, he jammed his knee into my crotch and moved it up and down.

"Ooh, I am enjoying that," I said, and then added, "Come on, make some room for me. You two are bloody enormous.

"We always get the impitent [sic] ones in here," said one of the men.

Finally I settled down, took out my tube of snuff and offered it around while I listened to a couple of the men finish off their conversation about a film that had been on television the previous night. Then one man who had noticed my strange accent asked me the inevitable question.

"Where do you come from?"

"Inverness."

"It's a long way from home. Are you a traveller or do you stay in Shields?"

I told him I stayed in South Shields in digs that cost me £16 a week. It astonished them. We talked about the cost of board and lodging and one man said it would be cheaper if I got digs in a village as opposed to a town. Another man said he had lived in a village for five years and had still not made a real friend among his neighbours.

"The trouble with the village is that they're over-clannish," he said.

After a while the interest in that subject waned and I was asked some more questions — what had been my job before I became a pitman and frankly what was I doing down a pit anyway? I gave out the familiar stream of patter about money. Then the cockney said, "I don't believe a word of it. I bet it's all because of a woman. You've put a bird in Inverness up the stick ain't yer?"

"No."

The cockney then told me that it was because of a woman that he had come to work down a pit. At the age of seventeen he had married a Geordie lass. She had hated living down south and so he had agreed to try living in the north. The only work going at the time was pitwork. He had been a Bevan boy.

That conversation petered out and there was silence for a while. Later I opened my haversack to get out a new tin of snuff and one of the men noticed my magazines. "Hey, you've got some porn mags. Let's have a quick shufti!"

When he took them out of my haversack he was astonished to see they were copies of the *Economist*. That prompted another of the men to say, "I've heard about you. You're the lad who recites poetry over the dac."

I explained I was romantically inclined and poetry released these romantic feelings. So that brought us on to the topic of sex again and whether I had a lass.

Then one of them told me the old-looking pitman seated on my right was getting married in three weeks' time. They said he was only twenty-nine years old. Nevertheless they said, he was a very old twenty-nine and might be past it. A young lad like me was exactly what he needed to help him out if things came unstuck on the night of his wedding. I replied I did not fancy helping him out with the sort of woman he was likely to marry.

The manset arrived at the landing and the older pitman, who was supposed to be only twenty-nine, turned to me and said quite seriously, "Could you give me a hand with this leg of mine. It's a bad 'un."

I told him if he was strong enough to get married by himself he was strong enough to get out of the manset by himself. But he insisted he needed help. So eventually I gave him a hand and after some trouble together we managed to get his faulty leg out of the manset. He then walked away without the slightest hint of a limp.

Yours, Kit

PS: Somebody came up to me the other day and asked me if I was Lord Lucan. I said, "Do I look like Lord Lucan?" He muttered something about plastic surgery.

Letter 13

Dear Teddy,

I am finding life more and more bizarre. Two odd things have recently happened — not down the pit but up above it.

A few weeks ago a couple moved in upstairs. At first I hardly saw them — not even at meal times — because they are self-catering. But recently I bumped into them in the Stag's Head, my local pub. As I strolled in, they gestured to me to come over and so I joined them at their table.

They are both small and in their late twenties — a slight and undistinguished couple that normally I would not notice. Of the two she did most of the talking, which I found surprising as it is the cultural norm here for the woman to say little, at least in front of the men. But it didn't seem to bother him. He was enjoying his pint and, if anything, he was positively encouraging us to talk.

We started by gossiping about the landlord and then I told her about the pit. After ten minutes I felt we had known one another for years. As the conversation proceeded I told her how I'd come down to South Shields and how at first I found life here so alien. She appeared fascinated and I felt much cheered.

Actually, when I think about it, she must be the first woman I have in any way properly spoken to since

I've been here. I found it a particular relief because I felt I did not have to conceal anything from her. She was completely unconnected with the pit and she was sympathetic to me. She was entirely different to the girls I normally come across here. It is impossible to talk to girls at a disco not just because of the noise but also because they are on their guard, especially against an unknown male quantity like myself with a funny way of talking, no swagger and a nose.

Eventually at closing time we made our way back to the digs and our respective rooms. Half an hour later on the way to the bathroom I saw her leaning on the staircase in tears. I was just about to say something when she shouldered past me still sobbing. Then her husband appeared. Avoiding my eyes, he too slipped down the staircase and followed her into the street. I found it all most perplexing, indeed even a little disturbing. Just half an hour before, we were happily chatting in the pub and then suddenly there is this disintegration. Perhaps I am reading too much into the situation but I find it highly suspicious that first they appear to sleep all day, second she is in tears, and third she is bundled out into the streets at 11 p.m. Teddy, I think I have met my first prostitute.

I'll never know though. Three days later I left the digs for good. I have now moved in with Irish John. His landlady had been looking for another lodger. Irish John told me about it and I jumped at the offer.

I waited till supper time on Thursday, the day before yesterday, before telling the landlord that I was moving out of his house the next day.

"Something wrong is there? Don't you like my cooking?"

"No, it's just that I will be moving in with a friend."

"Oh really, a friend," he said, stressing the last word. A homosexual! That's it, he probably thought. He had always known there was something wrong with me. Lodgers were all the same. If they were not on the run from the law they were invariably perverts. He went back to the kitchen, produced my meal, returned to the kitchen while I ate it, cleared it away and then told me to leave the room. He was locking up.

I replied that I wanted to watch the television. No, he said, I have to leave and he was going to lock up the sitting-room. I said I had paid rent until the following day so I was within my rights to use every facility in the house. I firmly plonked myself down in an armchair while he proceeded to remove the heater, the television, the lamp and every light bulb in the room. I said to him, "It is cold. It is dark. There is no television and yet I am going to stay right here in this armchair."

He threatened to call the police. I invited him to. Then he pounced. Brandishing his clenched fist with its glinting signet ring on his foremost finger, he shouted at my face from a distance of not more than three inches, "I'm going to fill you in if you don't get out of here!"

I offered no resistance but I said I was not moving. Then I gripped the seat of the armchair while he tried to wrestle me out of it. Finally he gave up and said, "Well, you can stay there all night for all I care."

"I will," I said, bringing out a cigar from my inside pocket and lighting it.

After a while he backed down and left me puffing away in the dark. I must have stayed there a good hour because I wanted to be sure he wasn't lurking in the kitchen just waiting for me to go to the pub. Eventually I did go to the pub. When I returned he was waiting for me at the top of the stairs. I was halfway up when I decided to turn back and forego brushing my teeth that night. Suddenly he leapt on me and bustled me down the stairs. My reaction was quite peculiar. I told him for some reason that he was doomed. I kept on repeating it. I could not think of anything else to say. I just went, "You're doomed! You're doomed!" Even after he left the house and I went to bed, I was still muttering, "He's doomed! He's doomed!"

Actually I suppose there is a vague explanation for this outburst of mine. I think I meant it as a comment on my landlord's attempts at self-improvement. Every so often over a pipe after my supper he used to sit down and confide in me about the unhappy state of his marriage. He said he loved his wife, but obviously that wasn't enough. Then one time he admitted that it might be his fault and he said he was trying to do something about himself. Then he produced his maxims — slips of paper, bound by sellotape to protect them — "You can take temptation so far before it becomes compulsion" and "What you get out of life is what you put in" and "Loving is giving in return" and so on.

Yours, Kit

Letter 14

Dear Teddy,

Last weekend — the first two full days with Irish John in my new digs — was a disaster.

I suppose in retrospect it was because we had nothing to distract us from each other and maybe we realized how shallow were our common experiences. Down the pit we see each other on the manset where we gossip and quip over a game of switch, together with a couple of other miners. The pit provides us with enough conversation for a couple of pints after work once or twice a week, but it cannot bridge the gap between us as we sit on either side of the gas fire during the weekend.

I tried to get a discussion going about Northern Ireland which, looking back on it, was risky in the extreme. After all, Irish John has on more than one occasion made muffled mention of his IRA connections and he is famous down the pit for the singing of his Republican songs.

I foolishly imagined that I could debate his point of view and in return he could give me the benefit of his first-hand experience of living in Ulster — or just outside it. Donegal is situated on the southern side of the Northern Ireland border. My opening question was to ask him to explain to me how good Irish Catholics, of which he was one, could blow up innocent children and square it with their consciences.

I had intended to soften the impact of this question by giving my reasons for putting it so brutally. He didn't allow me to continue because he suddenly went crazy. He became lethal. One more word from me and he would have taken my head and smashed it against the mantelpiece. It was as if a safety catch had been taken off his mind. I stayed put. Didn't breathe a word. He stood there letting off a stream of invective about how as an Englishman I didn't understand anything about Northern Ireland. That was exactly my point but I didn't dare make it.

The second incident occurred the following day, just when it looked as if we were recovering from the row. The landlord had taken us for a Sunday-morning pint. We came back feeling nice and mellow for the Sunday lunch his wife had prepared for us. Afterwards we staggered off to our sitting-room and Irish John suggested a game of Scrabble. Soon he was in great good spirits because he was getting higher scores than me. It prompted him to make a few jovial remarks about the worth of my education.

"Where are your precious A-levels now? They're no match for the little Irish brain that's ticking away in my head," he roared. "Everything I got in here, Chris boy, I got myself. No teacher put it there."

Then came the fateful moment when he managed to fit in the word "poxed". He was terrifically pleased with it because an "x" is worth eight points in the game and he had engineered it so that his "x" landed on a triple letter score. I told him to stop counting up his score because the word in that form did not exist in the English language. Of course it bloody did, he replied. That prompted me to say that just as one does not "mump" or "measle", so one does not pox. He was thrown by what I said, lost his temper and kicked the Scrabble board into the air. I have since discovered that I am in fact wrong.

The lads at work were astonished. We had left the pit on Friday the best of mates. Here we were on Monday, back for the nine in the morning shift in a state of silent mutual hostility. Then in the course of the shift, everybody got to hear our opposing versions of what had happened over the weekend.

My attitude is that we need time to get used to one another. The problem is that Irish John is the first non-bourgeois man I have attempted to have as a proper friend. I discount Harry and Owen from my days at Harlow Technical College. They might have spoken with broad accents and they might have preserved certain cultural practices inherited from their parents, but their education and their apprenticeship as trainee journalists made them in essence as bourgeois as the next man. No, Irish John is the genuine proletarian all right and, not surprisingly, we are running into difficulties.

I am getting a clearer idea about work at the coalface now. I reckon that when the machines are functioning properly and the roof is holding firm, then coalface work is a doddle. On a perfect shift, as I've said before, not only do most of the people at the face get a good two or three hours doing nothing, but the work they are called on to do would hardly tax a debutante.

The problem is when things begin to go wrong. For

example, last week we ran into crumbling roof at F55. This means that production has to stop while the job of wood dowelling is done. This is the heaviest job on the face. It involves drilling five-foot-long holes in the top of the wall into which are placed tubes of gell and hickory sticks. Two people are needed to hold the drill in place.

On Wednesday the overman, Arthur Vanackter, took me on the face to see if I could do it. I had begged him to let me have a go. Morris Givens was appointed to help me. We pointed the drill upwards, set the knob to start the five-foot-long drill rotating and the whole damned thing nearly jumped clean out of our hands. We managed to regain control of it. At first the drill holed into the wall quite nicely but then it got stuck. Whatever we tried it refused to go further in. Within five minutes my arms and back were in agony and I was relieved when Vanackter took my place.

Yours, Kit

Letter 15

Dear Teddy,

I had my first taste of industrial action last week and I fancy I acquitted myself with honour on the field of battle.

The dispute arose out of a difference of opinion over whether men should be moved from their cavil (place of work) in the middle of a shift. One of the concessions the NUM have won from the management is the stipulation that once a shift has started no man can be moved. This rule is insisted on for safety reasons. A man suddenly rushed to a new place of work, where he has never been before, is thought to be accident-prone. The manager argued this was a special case. The tailgate machine was too far in advance of the mulligate machine of F55 so the tailgate men had nothing to do. It was absurd to have a group of men spending a whole shift doing nothing when they could be helping men elsewhere, he said. So he ordered them to go and help the No. 10 minermen. They refused. Pay was docked.

My job on the stageloader at F55 face meant I was at the centre of the action. I spent the shift using the outside phone to ring up union officials on bank, using the dac to put the colliery overman in touch with developments and taking instructions from the face.

At the end I felt proud that I had contributed in no small way to the successful execution of the walk-out.

It was a hard-working shift for me but a fulfilling one. I relayed points of information to and fro, painstakingly remaining as objective as possible in my reporting. Even when at one point my conversation over the dac was being interrupted by beeping. I put the beeping down to underhand tactics by the management — or else it could have been Davy Glock. Glock is a nineteen-year-old punk employed on a button and he finds beeping a relieving diversion.

Anyway when they finally decided to walk out I made vocal agreement with the sentiment expressed by mulligate chockman Ronnie Ritchard when he said, "It's the right decision because if we all come out now, it will speed things up. They will know we mean business."

I was all for showing some worker solidarity and walking out but the face union man, Bobby Sparks, told me to shut up. As it happened the walk-out did not prove effective because it did not even win over the top union officials. Lodge secretary, Jim Inskip, said he would talk to the pit manager but the union would not authorize any industrial action. He advised the men to think again, which they did, and they were back at work the next day, having accepted the loss of the previous shift's earnings.

On the subject of Irish John I'm not sure our relationship has properly bottomed out although our initial high expectations of one another have long since been dashed. In their place has emerged a *modus vivendi* of sorts. We have fallen into a routine whereby our coexistence can proceed from one day to the next without either of us being sent into paroxysms of rage.

When I say either of us I really mean him because I have not yet mastered the art. With me it's all bubbling resentment.

To preserve this truce in our domestic relations I have found it necessary to skirt around Irish John's ego-hardened personality like a river around a rock. I avoid certain obviously dangerous subjects and give in to him whenever he asserts some opinion — even over the most trivial things. I have completely given up over the telly, which means I have to sit through hours and hours of "Hawaii 5–0" and "Charlie's Angels". He loves anything American. So it's western adventure stories for literature, US cops for television and steak and chips for supper. I have never had so much steak in my life.

We go shopping together on Saturday in the super-market. I push the trolley around and he bungs stuff in it. The first counter we make for is the fridge freezer where they stock jumbo bargain packs of chuck steaks. Second stop is the freezer where they keep the chips and we buy about a thousand of them. Funnily enough Irish John does all the cooking because he is most particular about how he likes his steak and his chips done and he couldn't possibly trust me to get it right.

I once bought myself an avocado pear, the ingredients for spaghetti carbonara and a yoghurt just to have a break from the relentless steak and chips. It was a battle enough in the supermarket, let alone when it came to supper time. I offered to split the avocado with him.

"Now, Chris, you can take that horrible green thing away from me. I didn't get to my present size without treating my digestive system with a degree of respect.

I've got an Irish stomach and it expects good Irish meat — or at least English-speaking meat if you get my drift — and nicely browned chips made from good Irish potatoes."

Since then I have reverted to his diet because it saves me the bother of having to cook, although I have persevered with my yoghurts. I need something sharp and bitter to break down the aftertaste of Irish John's fry-ups.

"And they say the Irish are thick! You wouldn't get me paying 13p for a pot of milk that's gone off."

We had a battle over eggs last Saturday. I took the liberty of leaving my post at the trolley and going over to the egg mound, picking up a box of half a dozen eggs and putting them in our trolley. On his peregrinations around the supermarket he also had acquired a packet of eggs. His eggs were cheaper. Mine were bigger. This was perfect. Here at last was a classic and beautifully simple example of how there can be two utterly plausible sides to even the most elementary arguments. How foolish it is for anyone to imagine that theirs is the only correct point of view. Surely Irish John could see that. I made an introductory remark to that effect, tactfully couched in general terms, so as to avoid any pointed reference to any failing he might have in this field of human discourse.

"I don't know what you're crapping on about, Chris," he said, "and I haven't got all day to stand around here and find out. Now I'll put your eggs back."

"Why? What's wrong with them?"

"They're more expensive."

"Ah, but they're bigger."

"You can hardly see the difference in the size."

"What's 4p?"

"It's pointless just throwing away money."

"But we'll hardly notice the money. It's such a tiny amount."

"Well if it's such a tiny amount, you buy those fucking eggs and I'll buy these ones. We'll buy our food separately."

"No, no. I don't care about the eggs."

"Well what have you been talking about then?"

"I was just trying to make a point about the nature of an argument."

"Look, if it's an argument you want I'll have you outside."

He always gets the last word. Always. I believe it's a real compulsion. There is probably a device in his ear which tells his brain to make a remark if the last one he hears in an exchange is not his own. This self-induced reflex action of his has, of course, made him a formidable opponent.

He has had a series of clashes with Don Pyle in the manset over such controversial matters as the correct pronunciation of the world "calibre". Is the emphasis on the "a" or the "i"? Then there was the raging argument about whether you could describe lager as a beer or whether lager is a lager as cider is a cider. You won't believe that he confided to me after that particular conflict of opinion. He said, "The problem about Don Pyle is that he always thinks he's right." I nearly blacked out.

By the way, I have taken up with a couple of lads called Geordie Stephenson and Tony Davis. They have recently been put on transport and this past week they have been taking materials inbye to the F55 mulligate, i.e. via my stageloader. So they take their main breaks with me. They are both very *sympatico*, as the Italians say, and they make a refreshing change from Irish John and many of the abrasive young lads I've met since I've been here. They are both married with a child apiece. They look about twenty-three. They have been transferred from another shift so they don't really know anybody on mine. I have invited them to our card school. A welcome injection of new blood for Irish John to work his charm on.

Yours, Kit

ps: I forgot to post this letter today. I'll just add what happened this morning. Irish John refused to walk to work with me because I had lavatory paper on my neck. I had nicked myself shaving in a couple of places and so I stuck on little bits of lavatory paper to staunch the bleeding. I mean, how ridiculous can you get?

Letter 16

Dear Teddy,

I have been finally promoted to transport but I won't tell you about my new job in this letter because right now I can think of nothing except what I am going to do about Irish John.

An incident has occurred which I simply cannot ignore. It bodes very ill for the future. But first I will give you the lead-up to the incident.

In the initial few days after I had introduced Geordie and Tony into our card school, it looked as if our relationship was rallying. He was impressed I could make such first-rate friends. They seemed genuinely to like and appreciate me.

For a while I felt him relax the tight vigil he kept on my person. Perhaps now we could look back at our troubled relationship and pick out and develop the positive elements so that our new affinity could, in time, become a firm and fully-fledged friendship.

The flimsy little thing barely lasted till the end of the week before it was put paid to by an unfortunate exchange over the breakfast table. I opened out the *Daily Mail* that was lying on the table and without stopping to think, I exclaimed, "Good God, that's my cousin!" It was a front-page piece about her alleged friendship with a nephew of the late President Kennedy.

"You fucking liar!"

I was temporarily confused and I blushed.

"What makes you want to act so bloody superior saying you're related to her," he said, "just 'cos she's got the same surname as you?"

"I was only kidding."

"Like hell you were."

In the shift that followed he spread it around the manset about what a lying snob I was. Obviously I am especially sensitive to any slander of that nature. The last thing I want is to be the sole butt of a class war down the pit. I couldn't respond to any of his jibes on that manset ride inbye. I just had to bear them in resentful silence.

On Monday I got my own back, not that I did it for reasons of revenge. I just saw it as a chance to have an easy shift. I woke up at 4 a.m., got dressed and felt my way downstairs. There was no sign of Irish John. He had his own alarm clock but either it had failed to go off or else he had slept through it. I decided not to wake him up. So I went to work by myself and had a lovely relaxed shift without having to put up with Irish John's overbearing presence.

That evening he was furious but I had a ready excuse. I said, as innocently as I could, that when I saw he had not appeared in the morning I had imagined that he had chosen to take a rest day (you get six paid rest days a year which you can take whenever you want) or else that he had chosen to lie in and was intending to go in a 9 a.m. shift.

"I'll do the same to you one day," he said.

I haven't mentioned it before but for some time it has been an accepted part of our rough and tumble relationship that Irish John playfully demonstrates his superior strength by twisting my arm or by putting my neck in an armlock and getting a quick exaggerated submission from me. This stopped when Geordie and Tony arrived in our carriage but now once again he has stepped up these "playful" attacks on me. He has taken to cracking and snapping my fingers, clouting me across the ear and, most painful of all, he now grabs me round the neck and rubs my head furiously with his knuckles. Nobody helps me out and, funnily enough, I hardly defend myself. I am behaving like a rabbit caught in the glare of a headlight. I am bewildered by what seems to be Irish John's irrational cruelty. Also I feel restricted in that we are supposed to be friends.

Already people are coming up to me and telling me that I should take a swing at him. My stock reply is that I am not violently inclined.

"You're just a bloody coward, mun."

"But he's a whole lot bigger than me."

"Bloody hit him in the face with a shovel then."

I have done nothing partly because I have to live in the same house as him and there are times, especially after one or two drinks, when the warmth of our old relationship returns. Second, I have been brought up to avoid losing my temper and never to punch a person. Third, there's the question of my teeth, so expensively put straight by my parents.

Anyway something had to be done and so the other day I decided not to sit next to him in the manset. I sat one bench away from him. Throughout the journey back to the shaft he made loud remarks about the fact that I was in a "huff". Eventually I answered by telling him to fuck off. The anger shot to his face and I can still see how unpleasant was the expression on his face when he said, "I would like to get you really annoyed because I would love to fill you in for serious."

Not long after that revealing outburst, we had an extended bait stop during which I was strongly advised to take some retaliatory action against Irish John. There were about five or six of us sitting in a circle of chocknobs and stonedust bags, discussing what I should do.

"Burst his bastard neck open!"

"Easier said than done. He's about one and a half times my size."

"Why, he's nothing, mun. He's soft right through."

"You know that's not true."

"What you want to do is to ask him whether he's got a handkerchief."

"A handkerchief?"

"Aye, for to carry his teeth home in after you've knocked them out!"

"Look, Stevie, I'm just not the violent type. I object to it on principle."

"Object to it on principle! My arse! It's just that you're too small to be violent."

"Why, don't be pathetic, Chrissy mun. You are sounding like that lad at school. You na, the little lad who told us how he survived all his beatings. He said, 'I curl up in a ball and wait until they have finished hitting me.'"

And that got them on to their fight stories. In fact they were soon enjoying themselves so much telling one another their stories that they forgot about my dilemma. The most vocal of them all was this lad called Paul from another shift, whom we didn't know, so nobody had heard his stories before. He told us about the staring game he played with his mates. Apparently you go to a pub and stare at somebody. If the lad on whom you have fixed your unblinking eyes looks away, you can console yourself with the assumption that you are harder than him. Should he have the impertinence to stare back at you, it is up to you to take the matter further. You simply ask the lad why he is staring at you and whether he is looking for a fight or something.

Paul concluded by saying, "Mind, I don't go in for that staring very much. I don't really like fighting. It's just that when you've got to fill a lad in, you have just got to get on with it."

Whether Paul enjoyed winning a fight or not, it was transparent he hated losing one under whatever circumstances. He told us how one night he was walking back from the pub with his girlfriend, his two mates and their two girlfriends. They had all had too much to drink, especially the lads. Three other lads started throwing fried chips at them. Paul could not possibly allow this sort of affront to his dignity to go unnoticed — especially with the lasses looking on. Threats were exchanged. The fight began. Paul and one of his mates were badly beaten up. The other mate fled. The lasses screamed. Paul felt paralysed with humiliation. What kind of hard man has fried chips thrown at him, is beaten in an equal fight and has a coward for a mate — and all this happening in front of his lass.

A couple of nights later, having sufficiently recovered from his bumps and bruises and having discovered the names and addresses of their three assailants, Paul and his good mate went on a little tour. They visited the first house on the list, knocked on the door and politely asked to speak to the lad they were looking for. The moment the lad got to the doorstep to see who was there, they pulled him out of the house and soundly beat him up. They did this to all three lads and also to the mate who had run away.

This started Stevie Wade and Davy Glock on their stories about the hard men of South Shields, notably Kevin Ringer, but I had heard most of these stories before, as had everybody else. Still they lose nothing in the repeating. Ringer is proud of his dog. He has trained it to be vicious by alternately petting it and hitting it. One day Ringer was out walking his dog. It would be wrong to imagine that this simple operation was conducted in the conventional manner — dog padding along at the heel of master. No, the dog charges off into the middle distance and from time to time in the course of the walk, dog and master meet up. On this particular day Ringer walked around a street corner and saw his dog being kicked by a gang of youths. Ringer marched up to the biggest of the lads and shouted, "What the fuck do you think you are doing?"

"But it attacked me."

"Don't give me that. The dog is docile."

Ringer knocked the lad down with a punch to the chin and then said, "And that means quiet."

Quite often I have heard stories from people who have

76

stood up to Ringer. The landlord of the Stag's Head once refused to sell him a drink. He could do very nicely without the custom of Ringer and his cronies, he had said. Ringer left without saying a word. Five minutes later the pub window that looked out on to the main street was smashed.

Inevitably a man of Ringer's notoriety becomes the subject of a host of rumours whose veracity is questionable. I have heard that he took over the managership of the up and coming South Shields punk rock group the Angelic Upstarts by frightening off the old manager, that he ran a protection racket in the town, that he was responsible for the three-year imprisonment of a man and that the police have no intention of pressing charges in the event of the man exacting a physical revenge on him. I heard that a couple of years back Ringer's house was set on fire and that negotiations to hire a hitman from Glasgow to kill him have only recently fallen through.

Some people say that he is a "vicious bastard" and that one day he will get his just desserts. Others, like Davy Glock and Stevie Wade, think that he is "a canny lad" once you get to know him.

There are other lesser-known hard men in the town who are as physically powerful and perhaps as vicious but maybe they don't have Ringer's personality. There is a woman who once walked into the urinal of a pub and calmly pissed all over a man who was so frightened that he did not move. Davy Glock had been in the urinal at the time and when he saw what was happening, he bolted for the door and escaped.

There is Bulldog Barber, who, feeling the urge to pick up a young lad called Davy Waggit and throw him into a nearby pond, did exactly that. He had never seen Waggit before in his life. Waggit got out of the pond and fled.

Finally there is John McGlashan. Rumour has it that Ringer has backed down to McGlashan twice.

So, as you see, there is quite a precedent for me to come out and have a fight with Irish John. There is a chorus of people just willing me to have a good crack at him. But there is always the age-old question to which, if you have no answer, you have no choice but to keep your fists in your pockets. What do you do if you are weaker than your opponent?

Yours, Kit

PS: I feel like Poland, which by virtue of its geographic situation, is forced to cope as best it can in the shadow of its powerful neighbour. That is I share digs with him, so I feel my freedom of speech curtailed. The truth I commit to paper late at night in the secrecy of my room (cf. underground press) and post to you. All is calm on the surface but underneath there stirs resentment. One day I will break free of my chains — although somehow I can't actually think of a way at the moment without quitting these comfortable digs and having to go through the upheaval of finding new ones (cf. defection) — but in the meantime I have to toe the party line.

Letter 17

Dear Teddy,

I feel awful. I feel utterly imprisoned by Irish John. I am even imprisoned when I am away from him. This I will explain after I have first told you what it is like to live with someone who is oppressing you.

Sometimes, like now, I am amazed at how quickly friendship has turned into a stranglehold. At other times, when the air is temporarily clear, I think our friendship can recover. I grin at the slightest positive remark, just to say it's all right, no hard feelings, it's never too late. Maybe he will concede a smile of sorts in response but then the pendulum swings back and another even lower point in the deterioration of our relationship is plotted. And at that point I wonder how on earth I got on with him so well before; how daring I must once have been when now I am stuck for anything to say.

By myself, I sit staring at nothing in particular, mulling over his barbs and insults from our infrequent exchanges. I try this answer and that in place of the makeshift one I gave at the time. I try and prepare myself for the next exchange so that I won't be caught again but I am always disarmed by the cruelty that I see ignited in his black eyes that are really blue.

I feel pinched and confined by this relentless fourteen-stone presence in the house. He sits on the other side of the gas fire with his great single-track mind, sometimes bunched in a tight ball of prejudice and at other times jumping up and down like a jack-in-the-box, always fluent and certain. And here am I, a bundle of uncertainties and complications and so dumb. At the root of it, I suppose, we no longer properly communicate because neither of us respects the other; he is contemptuous of my apparent weakness, my inability to retaliate; and I despise him because he is so unreasonable.

When he is in the grip of a burst of temper, I don't see him as a rational person. What I see is a chemical thing, for which he needs an antidote, a drug. There must be some chemical periodically released in his brain which causes it to press against the roof of his head and send him into a fury. The other day he said he was annoyed, almost in a whining, complaining voice, as if he was blaming me for annoying him and so activating his temper, over which — beyond a certain point — he has no control.

I might be getting a bit pretentious here but I wonder if there is not really a direct and intimate connection between an oppressor and his victim. They see right through to the soft core of each other. The weakness in Irish John that I see is his lack of control. It is like an addiction. It is as if he cannot help himself. If I cross him, he finds himself locked in a state of mind that brings him to the brink of violence. Maybe it is tantalizing for him that he does not actually go over the edge because I invariably back down and that is my weakness. I can imagine that it is the prospect of violence that gives him the taste of something sweet and putrid and exciting. The act of violence, I suppose, is a kind of orgasm.

I feel tired and depressed. When I wake up in the morning there is a blissful moment before I have gathered my senses and properly focused my mind for the day. It is like having a cold. You wake up and you don't know if you have still got it. So you give a couple of tentative sniffs and you discover it's still there. Capstan Full Strength.

You know, I bet there are a lot of Geordie housewives who feel like me for the most part of their married lives. I can imagine quite a few of the people I know down the pit being pretty tyrannical at home. You know, D. H. Lawrence *Sons and Lovers*. All that sort of thing.

It was the imprisonment of my spirits that I am suffering at the hands of Irish John that prompted me to fix up a free weekend away from him — an ironical pretext it turned out.

The plan was to meet my two brothers, Alastair and Anselm, at Leicester train station last Friday at 7 p.m. Unfortunately, I caught the wrong train by mistake and arrived two hours late. Neither of my brothers was there. They had assumed after an hour and a half of waiting that for some reason I wasn't coming. I had no way of contacting them. Alastair doesn't have a telephone. So I went into the nearest pub and got talking to a couple of lads, one of whom offered to put me up for the night on the floor of his flat. They both lived in the same block of flats. So about 11.30 p.m., after closing time, the three of us started to walk to their block of flats. We had just got to the entrance when a car screeched to a halt and three tough men charged up the steps.

They challenged us, asking for our names in an aggressive manner. Two of us meekly gave our names but Pete answered them vehemently: "What's it got to do with you what my name is?"

They pushed him back and said they were the police. As they were not in uniform Pete asked them to prove it. By this time one of them had him in an armlock. I tried to intervene but was grabbed myself by another of the policemen who asked me for my name as well. I said I had already given my name. He then pulled me down and held me by the neck in a tight armlock and he told me not to give him "any college-boy lip".

I replied that now I certainly refused to give my name for the second time until I was released from the armlock. He just tightened his grip and said that it was serious. They were looking for a child-killer. I could not see how my name was going to help them find him. From that exchange you can see how mutually irritating we were — that is, the policemen and myself

Police cars arrived and I was bundled down the steps to one of them. I saw my mate on the ground being kicked by two policemen and generally roughed up.

We were driven to the police station and I heard the policeman in front say into his dac or intercom that he had arrested two lads for assault. But at the police station I was informed that I was being done for a breach of the peace. Then I was taken away to a police cell for the night. At about three in the morning I was visited by two of our plain-clothed policemen. This time they were quite friendly and one of them said cheerily, "Well, Chris, you had a few jars last night. Caused a bit of a rumpus, didn't you?"

"No."

"Come on. Don't be stubborn. Just sign here admitting you were in breach of the peace and that'll be the end of it."

It occurred to me they could beat me up in this little cell and no one would be the wiser, but on balance I didn't think they would. Anyway I said, "If there's anybody who is guilty of anything, it is you, not me." Or maybe I didn't say that. Maybe I just said, "Look, I didn't do anything and you know perfectly well I didn't." At least, whatever I did actually say must have persuaded them that I didn't commit a breach of the peace because by nine o'clock that morning they had changed the charge to obstruction. Obviously I have pleaded not guilty to that as well. A trial date has been set for both me and my mate for a couple of weeks' time.

I will finish this letter now because it is long enough and I'll carry straight on to my next letter which will be all about my new job on transport.

Yours, Kit

Letter 18

Dear Teddy,

Here I am again, Teddy, one minute later. I will put these letters in separate envelopes too. Don't you agree that the best part of getting letters is opening envelopes?

Now, just a quick introductory paragraph about transport work before I start telling you how hard or dangerous it is. A coalmine needs various materials to expand underground such as: steel girders, air bags, belt structure, all sorts of different types of timber, etc. All these are loaded on bank on to trams which are then lowered in a cage down the shaft. From here they are pulled by the loco (underground train) four miles to a central landing. The transport lads then take them, by means of tuggers and haulage ropes, nearer the coalface.

Certainly if you ask a pitman who has the most arduous job in the pit he will probably cite the transport lad but, in actual fact, it depends on the shift. You can have an easy shift loading light timber and belt structure, or you can have a "rough un" offloading girders, pipes, rails and crown props or rerailing trams.

It also depends on the squad of lads you are working with. Some are out to get away with doing the absolute minimum and others are conscientious. In our shift of a dozen lads there is only one who is truly idle.

(As a matter of course we are all called a bunch of idle bastards by our colliery overman, Jim Casey.) After the slothful Kennie, I am probably the least hardworking lad because there are occasions in every shift when my incompetence prevents me from taking a fully active role.

I have mastered the theory all right. It is the dirty, jagged practice that throws me. I'll give you the theory. There is kinetics, which we were taught at Seaham. Kinetics is the science of picking things up without overstraining yourself. There are two golden rules. First, you should use leverage whenever you can and second, it is imperative that you keep a straight back when lifting. That way you use the power of your calf muscles and you won't put your back out of joint.

There is a total fallacy about carrying. It is an erroneous belief that the easiest way for two people to carry something long, like an arched girder, is on their shoulders. That is as sensible as telling housewives to carry their wash baskets balanced on their heads. There are Africans who presumably have got the necessary flat-topped heads and an exquisite sense of balance; similarly there might exist working men with steel-rimmed shoulder blades. However for the normal chap such as myself whose head is coconut-shaped and whose shoulder is a patchwork of knobbly bones, it is murder. Nevertheless there *is* a bit of the body that is tailor-made for the job. It is the wadge of flesh you will find just above the hip. Curiously it is comfortable and in this position the weight is taken by the legs, making the means of transport kinetically sound.

If you are good at carrying pianos upstairs or extricating cars from ditches, you are just the man needed for transport down the pit. Unfortunately those are precisely the abilities I lack, so that although I work well at the simple jobs such as loading and offloading trams or putting things into piles, when anything becomes complicated I just get in the way.

At its most difficult transport work requires ingenuity. Unlike coalface and tunnel work, there have been no revolutionary post-war innovations to make it easier. The step from pit ponies to trams was taken in the first half of the century and that is as far as progress has got in this field. In fact the method they use to move a chock is identical to that used in the days of the pyramids. Employing pull-lifts and sylvesters, the chock is pulled along on splits and crown props, which serve as wooden rollers.

Basically all the equipment a transport lad uses is a tram, a shifter and a hack. At Westoe you have to go searching for your hack at the beginning of a shift. Pieces of loose equipment like hacks, shovels, mells and saws are hidden all over the pit. There are only two tool lockers in our district. The suppliesman has the key to one and the greaser has the key to the other. The transport lads don't have any keys. So it means that at the end of a shift each squad of transport lads has to hide its tools. A naturalist knows where to look for birds' nests, similarly anybody who has been on transport for a while knows where to look for hidden gear. It is found at the side of refuge holes, on timber in the roof and in a pile of unused belt structure. The other day we did a hundred-yard methodical girder-by-girder search of the roadway from the beginning of the top landing to the first set of air doors. Three of us found seven hacks and one mell.

How dangerous is transport work? Of all the jobs down the pit, it has the highest casualty rate. Over half the people killed in accidents down the pit in Britain last year were transport lads: twenty-five of forty-eight. This is because trams are lethal. A runaway tram will kill anybody who gets in its way. Also you are not so protected from a fall of roof because you are not always under a massive steel chock. If a boulder comes loose from the roof in between the steel girders and falls on you you might be maimed, even killed.

This doesn't mean to say that transport work in the mines is the most dangerous in Britain. There are more fatal injuries in agriculture than in coalmining. I would say, however, that minor injuries on transport occur frequently and there are many near-accidents. The other day I almost lost a leg by the trip button at the bottom of a slope leading up to the 75G button. Foolishly I was standing too near the rails. Suddenly the sheckles of the haulage rope struck the axle of a nearby tram of girders, propelling it forward. It was plunging towards the back of my leg when Geordie shouted and, just in time, I jumped from its path.

On another occasion I was sitting on an empty tram leaning on my right arm with my hand clasped around the edge. Suddenly the metal structure of the belt grazed the side. It was a sheer fluke I decided to scratch my nose when I did. Otherwise I would have lost my fingers.

My hands are always getting cut and bruised. I have had black blood clotting under the skin where I have been nipped by a trip button. They have been blistered, ripped, scarred, scabbed. I swing the hack to hit the star of a clip, miss and bash below my knee. I get skin between thumb and forefinger nipped in the join of a star clip. Girders are constantly cutting me. I bleed on maybe two shifts out of five. Often it does not hurt. I suppose it is because I'm a beginner and my hands are so soft compared to other miners. Pushing a pen is no training for the pit.

The only job comparable to transport is tunnel work, which may not be as hard but is probably as dangerous. Tunnels are made by development workers with huge excavating machines called Doscos or Miners. Tunnels are driven to open up new faces. The dangers to development workers are falls of roof. Unlike the facemen, they are not protected by steel chocks. Indeed before they erect the girders, somebody has to poke the newly cut roof with a long pole to dislodge any loose boulders. At the tailgate of F56 I saw a roof-fall big enough to have buried somebody. Luckily the tunnelling squad were having their bait at the time.

Where there is stone in the way of a developing tunnel, explosives are sometimes used. Only an official is allowed to handle explosives and it is his job to make sure that there is nobody within a certain distance. Still, even from quite a way back you feel the blast. Sometimes the charge is so powerful that distant air doors are blown wide open.

At the No. 10 developments where we transport

materials they have to use dynamite at least three times a shift. Hands over my ears, I crouch behind a tram or in a refuge hole, peeping round only to ask No. 10 overman Colin Turnbull, "How many more seconds until the bomb goes off?"

He just sits there hovering over the plunger. The actual explosion is never as loud as I think it will be. It is the suspense that gets me. It is like waiting for your next hiccough.

Yours, Kit

Letter 19

Dear Teddy,

A few days ago I sold Irish John a watch for £3. That was Wednesday. It is now Saturday. When the transaction took place we agreed on a two-day guarantee so that if the watch had ceased to work by midnight on Friday, I would return his money.

Next day he took the watch down the pit. I did not see him until the end of the shift because he works in a different part of the district. One of the first things he did when he clambered into the manset was to shout to me across two rows of people that he wanted his £3 back. I asked why.

"The fucking watch has stopped. That's why."

"Let's have a look then."

"It's ticking at the moment. The point is that it stopped for half an hour in the middle of the shift. It's unreliable."

"But it's ticking at the moment, is it?"

"Oh aye, it's ticking now but it's no fucking good."

"Oh well, as long as it's ticking, then it's still working and our agreement is that if it is still working by midnight on Friday, I keep the money and you —"

"Don't you fucking play games with me, mate. You just hand over —"

"Look, if it's still bloody ticking —"

"I'll soon stop it bloody ticking. I'll fucking jump on the cunt."

"That's wrong and you know it's wrong. The agreement is —"

"The agreement is that if you don't hand back that money I'll fucking dismantle your overgrown features."

"You can threaten me as much as you like but on a question of principle I will not budge."

"Fucking budge! By the time I have finished with you, you won't be *able* to budge!"

Everybody in our carriage of the manset seemed to be laughing and cheering either Irish John or myself. The older pitmen are always amused by young lads arguing. There were shouts of, "That's it, Paddy, you tell him" and "You bloody well stick to your guns, Chris!"

"You're an ignorant Irish pig!" I screamed. "You're a stupid big-nosed cunt!" he shouted back. But after a few minutes they got bored and we were told to shut up, which we eventually did.

It so happened that at the shaft while we were waiting for the cage, I found myself standing in the queue just one or two men away from Irish John. I was talking to Stevie Wade and Ronnie Ritchard. I told them that I had had only one fight before in my life and that was when I was twelve.

"I don't think it will be long before you have your second one," said Stevie.

"Yes, I should have spent more time training," I said. "Ronnie was teaching me how to set about hitting Paddy."

Irish John turned and shouted at my face, "Don't talk about me behind my back to other people!"

"Look, if I want to, I will."

"If I tell you not to, you fucking well will not!" he said, pinching my cheek and jabbing me with his forefinger.

I suddenly lost control of myself and I punched him smack on the chin. He fell back for a moment and he said, "Right, you have really asked for it now and you are going to get it!"

Immediately a space was made for us. Irish John gave his haversack for somebody to hold. I had already dropped mine. Within a few seconds I had taken another swing at him and missed — and he had punched me in the face, knocking my helmet off my head and me almost off balance. I remember shouting at him, "You'll never get that three pounds back! Never! Not ever! As a matter of principle!"

Another couple of blows were exchanged before we were pulled apart by some older pitmen. The fight could not have taken longer than ten seconds but I was shaking for at least ten minutes afterwards.

In the showers everyone was talking about the fight and several people came up to congratulate me. I was called Chrissy Spinks by an electrician (after Leon Spinks, who defeated Muhammad Ali in the World Heavyweight Championship).

It occurred to me then that I had done a lot of people a favour. Admittedly, of all the people in the shift, I was the one who suffered most from him but there were quite a few others who had felt the sharpness of his tongue.

I was enjoying the reception from the fans until somebody asked where I was going to fight Irish John properly. Outside the canteen? At the back of the wages office?

That wiped the smile off my face. I thought I had done what was expected of me. But the lad explained that the business was only half finished. We had been prevented from really damaging one another down the pit, where it was a sackable offence to be caught fighting, but on bank there were no restrictions. The ghastly over-talkative chap went on. He said that nobody had actually won the fight. Others agreed and somebody else ventured that Irish John was probably waiting for me outside the canteen right now. If I did not present myself he would be able to say I had backed out.

I quickly got changed and looked for Irish John but I couldn't find him. I eventually saw him walking fifty yards in front of me up the street to the digs. I ran after him and, in a purposely unprovocative voice, asked him whether he wanted to finish the fight. I suggested the public gardens as being a suitable venue. He told me to bugger off. I did not want to press the point but I thought I had to ask him one more time because he had not directly answered my challenge. I don't think anybody has ever been invited to a fight in a more inoffensive and frankly ingratiating way. From the tone of my voice, I could have been inviting him to a party. He was still angry. Nevertheless it is to his eternal credit that he replied he would not condescend to fight me because such a conflict would result in my annihilation. It would be no contest. I almost felt like congratulating him on his astuteness in bringing up the very point that had been worrying me and, furthermore, on coming to the same conclusion.

Since then we have not exchanged a word. We went to different pubs last night and this morning we ate breakfast together in silence. It is now lunchtime and I'm going to nip out for a stroll round the town and a beefburger.

Yours, Kit

Letter 20

Dear Teddy,

The landlady has told both Irish John and myself to go and look for new lodgings. The reason she gives is that she has just sold the house but I haven't seen any "For Sale" boards in the front garden and, up until now, there has been no talk of selling.

I think it is just a ruse to get rid of us. It must have been obvious for some weeks that Irish John and I are not getting on and presumably they don't want to have to put up with bad feeling in the house.

Oh, and another thing: I suppose I ought to mention that in the end I gave Irish John his £3 back. I could not stand sitting beside him watching television night after night in complete stony silence. He kept it up for the whole of Saturday night. Neither of us went out. We just sat there on either side of the gas fire looking blankly at the Saturday-night western. Not a word was said.

Down the pit on Thursday we were treated to a visit by the manager. It is the first time I have seen him and it was quite a sight. Naturally we had all been warned of his impending visit so I knew who he was when he did eventually come. Otherwise I might have mistaken him for a cabinet minister or even the NCB Chairman. He had his own special white manset carriage which was the only one the loco was pulling. When it came to a halt at the manset landing a blaze of bright orange hit the eye as the manager, in smart new overalls, stepped out of the carriage, surrounded by his group of fellow travellers similarly attired. Not one of them was under the rank of colliery overman. It was like seeing Caesar with his Praetorian Guard. You were dazzled by the gleam of the jangling silver lamps and the clatter of the official yardsticks. It was a veritable cabinet of pit power. And then, suddenly, you knew you were in the presence of the Great Man for he was distinguished by his own special stick, the knob of which was shaped like a miniature pickhead, made out of genuine silver.

While I am on the subject of our management, I might as well tell you about our colliery overman, our overman and the deputy who supervises us transport lads in the North Main district. This will give you an idea of the quality of our immediate management.

First, there is our big Irish colliery overman, Jim Casey. Some bright spark gave him the nickname Domestos because he's strong and thick and clean round the bend.

There is a picture of Casey in my mind that will never fade. It is of him shouting at about ten people — eight transport lads and two powerloaders. Up at the No. 10 developments we were all working together pulling a heavy electricity cable. We needed to get it round a corner and Casey had ordered a couple of lads to move a pile of stonedust bags that were stacked where he wanted to have the cable. As the stonedust bags were being moved, he noticed that several of them were split so that stonedust was spilling out. He asked which squad of transport lads had been responsible for stacking the stonedust bags in the first place. Nobody answered.

That infuriated him and he raged about how useless we were and how stonedust bags do not grow on trees and how, in fact, they cost 50p a bag and what a joke it was that our union was putting in for a 40% pay claim because we were not even worth 40% of the wage we were getting at the moment. A squad of professional vandals would have stacked those stonedust bags with more care, he roared.

It was like listening to a Sergeant-Major walking up and down a line of soldiers bawling his head off with nobody moving, not even to scratch his nose, because that would only serve to localize the man's fury. I think Casey took some rueful pleasure from it because eventually he bellowed, "Transport lads. Why, I have them in my sandwiches for bait!"

Mind you, he has met his match in Davy Glock, a nineteen-year-old blond-streaked punk rocker who is totally indifferent to figures of authority. When Casey once told him to do something that he found unreasonable, his considered response was "Go fuck your nana." Casey was speechless.

On another occasion he actually walked out of the pit rather than work as a button lad as Casey had ordered him. Glock said he was caviled as a transport boy to F55 tailgate and so that was where he was going to stay, otherwise he was leaving. That episode resulted in another little chat with the manager and Glock found himself employed as a button lad for the next couple of weeks.

Then there was the time Casey ordered him to pick up all the bits of bait paper that were strewn about the F55 tailgate. Glock did not answer. Casey did not press his demand. He presumed Glock would do as he was told in his own good time and with his customary ill grace. Much later in the shift Casey happened to be walking that way again and he noticed that not one piece of paper had been picked up.

"Look here, Glock, when I tell you to pick up paper, that is exactly what I mean," boomed Casey. Glock glanced at him idly. Casey continued, "Do you think I talk just to keep my lips warm?"

"Na."

"Well then, get off your arse and clear this place up."

"Na."

"What do you mean — 'na'?"

"I mean I am a transport lad. As I see it, my job is to run trains and to load and offload girdas and timba. It is certainly not my job to hump fucking litta."

Within a trice Casey had Glock on his hands and knees picking up the paper. Glock got his own back. He nearly always did. The next shift there appeared a slogan inscribed in chalk on one of the big fourteen-foot straight-roof girders down at the Fourways. In large letters it read, "If brains were taxed, Casey would be in for a rebate."

Anybody can apply for his deputy's tickets as long as he has had at least two years' experience on the coalface; but it would be a foolhardy man indeed who puts himself forward to take the exams without having also the necessary leadership qualities. Among the lads I work with there are, in my opinion, four natural leaders. Two of them — Geordie Stephenson and Stevie Wade — have already been approached by an official to see if they are interested in going for their deputy's tickets once they have completed two years on the coalface. And they have four or five years to go before even being considered for face training. With that sort of forward planning and astute judgement, it is little wonder that we have such excellent deputies and overmen.

In our shift we have an overman and a deputy who are opposites and yet both are superlative managers of men. Overman Colin Turnbull has a reputation for having been a hard man in his younger days and that quality remains. I would not like to see him angry. He snaps occasionally but his expression of disapproval is enough to make most miners do what he wants.

Deputy Geordie Smith is built like a steel girder, but his face looks like a happy pineapple. He is full of mischief and laughter and gossip and consideration. I remember what he said to one of the lads who had just left his wife for his "bit on the side". Referring to the lad's girlfriend he said, "She might be nice, but I bet your wife is nicer." It was charmingly put. Then, as an afterthought he added, "You want to ditch this tart and go back to your wife while there's still time."

Geordie Smith is fortunate in that he has a warm giving personality which makes it natural for him to be liberal with praise and encouragement, so everybody likes working for him. He leads by example, always joining in wherever he is. And somehow he makes you work much harder though you don't realize it until he has left for some other part of the pit, and a job that you know normally takes an hour has taken only twenty minutes. Of course it helps him being so strong. In my first week as a transport lad, he told me to help him carry a fourteen-foot arched girder.

"Chris'll never carry that," exclaimed one of the lads. "He's far too bloody weak."

I had to agree. The last time I had attempted the feat my legs had buckled after barely half a dozen steps. But Geordie insisted. I was to take one end of the girder on my shoulder and he was to take the other. This was going to be humiliating, I thought, but it was quite the reverse because Geordie took the whole weight of the girder on his shoulder leaving me to traipse effortlessly along behind him. The lads were amazed at my apparent strength. That's the way to get loyalty.

Yours, Kit

PS: Forthcoming attractions over the next fortnight: my court case, Durham Miners' Gala and the search for new lodgings.

Letter 21

Dear Teddy,

British Justice has let me down. I was counting on it righting the wrong perpetrated against my person, not to mention that of my mate, by the British police. Incredibly, last week at the Leicester Magistrates Court, we were both found guilty. I was fined £50 and my mate £500. That's him temporarily ruined because the case has also cost him his job with the Post Office.

My court case has been a great subject of conversation down the pit, especially as I was well-known among the lads for maintaining that the British police were the finest in the world. This, of course, made them roar with laughter because quite a few men have had first-hand experience. I have come across several lads who have been arrested for joyriding, theft or breach of the peace. One or two of them have been in Borstal. I used to tell them that if they hadn't broken the law they wouldn't have such a jaundiced view of the police. I am, I said, perfectly prepared to admit that there are a few corrupt and brutal policemen but feel that, on the whole, they perform their difficult job with a basic rough honesty. This is where our views differ because the chorus of opinion from the lads is that, by and large, the police are corrupt.

"If you see a policeman at night, don't stop to answer questions, don't give any lip, don't try and be clever," said Glock. "Just quietly about turn and walk in the opposite direction. If necessary, run."

As it happens, I should have taken Glock's advice. He laughed his head off when he heard what had happened to me in Leicester. In fact, they were all mightily amused. There is nothing like a personal experience to support your point of view. Nevertheless I stood my ground with dignity. I said that I had just had the misfortune to come up against three dud policemen. I still maintain that there is nothing wrong with most of the constabulary.

They, however, ask what makes a man become a policeman when he knows just about every night of his working life he is going to be involved in ugly scenes: ordering people about, breaking up fights, restraining drunks? And what about the temptation and opportunity to lie, accept bribes and commit acts of violence once you are a policeman?

They were further amused when I said I had pleaded "not guilty". I was only heading for a bigger fine, they laughed. If it is possible to be wrongly arrested by the odd dodgy copper, I replied with suitable hauteur, this injustice will not escape the notice of the judiciary and the appropriate action will be taken. I gave them Habeas Corpus. I gave them the Magna Carta. We would, I answered them, not be disappointed by Leicester Magistrates Court.

The evidence of the three policemen was perfectly synchronized: each in turn solemnly stated that at this point the accused, Fraser, said he didn't do nuffing. Double negs. It's just not me. Let alone the cockney accent. My solicitor, courtesy of Legal Aid, must have felt the discrepancy too trivial to bother the magistrates with because he made no mention of it. Nor did he point out the more serious distortion of their evidence when one of the policemen was caught out lying.

We were astonished to see our homosexual friend appear as a prosecution witness, but at least he admitted that one of the policemen had had me by the neck in an armlock. The policeman in question was asked whether this had been so and he answered that he had not laid a finger on me. My solicitor asked him again but the policeman only repeated his lie. Perhaps my solicitor thought the contradiction in evidence between these two police witnesses was self-evident and so it needed no reference from him. But I think it was a mistake.

In his summing-up speech the prosecution barrister, a QC, said that in the course of the trial the bench had been presented with two conflicting stories. They had to make up their minds whose version of events they were going to believe. They could accept either the story of the two accused — both of whom had admitted they had been drinking on the night in question and one of whom had been swearing — or that of the police.

Once the magistrates had announced their decision to fine me £50, I stood up and asked them whether I could say something. There was a brief commotion and I was given permission. I said I was in a dreadful quandary. How could I pay this fine without committing perjury? Payment of a fine would mean an admission of guilt but that would be a lie because I was innocent. So, regretfully, I had to inform the court that I refused to pay. Their reply was to give me twenty-eight days in which to come up with the fine.

I returned to the pit full of fine rhetoric. And the countdown has begun. Twenty days, and then prisonwards I go with my head held high, my principles as bright and shiny as the stars in the heavens and my fellow workmates pissing themselves.

Now for the two other items of news I promised you at the end of my last letter. I have moved into new lodgings where there is a widowed landlady who cooks me meals and a lodger who is almost certainly homosexual. He has got extremely regular features and earns his keep as a nurse. The digs aren't half as comfortable as the ones I have just left but at least I am free of Irish John.

Last week I attended the Durham Miners' Gala which was, I am sad to report, a great anti-climax. I had dreamed of the Labour Party leader, swathed in red flags, being carried shoulder-high through phalanxes of heaving, cheering Geordie pitmen. I was expecting more from the City of Durham's famous Gypsy Green which I thought was going to be a cauldron of socialist fervour. I thought the Durham Miners' Gala was the occasion when the British Labour Party and the British trade union movement renewed their unshakeable faith in one another and demonstrated their dedication to the cause of the British worker as represented in its ultimate form — the Geordie coalminer.

In reality, while a good many people were enjoying themselves at the fun fair which occupied half Gypsy Green, the few who did gather to see what Jim Callaghan looked like in the flesh were hardly in a state of feverish excitement. The cheer he got when he mounted the podium was no more rapturous than a welcome at a village green fête.

Licking lollipops, they heard what the Labour Party leader had to say. He triumphantly informed this vaguely curious audience of how he had insisted on the postponement of the vital Bonn summit meeting, which had been specially called by the heads of state of the most powerful countries in the capitalist world to discuss how to accelerate the growth of the world economy and reduce their joint seventeen million unemployed. And the reason for the postponement? The date of the proposed summit meeting clashed with the Durham Miners' Gala! Poor Callaghan. That devastating revelation did not even earn him a clap!

The Durham Miners' Gala is now nothing more than a diverting day out with the family and not a very popular one at that. During the parade through the streets of Durham, only fifty out of the two thousand Westoe miners marched behind their lodge banner.

Yours, Kit

Letter 22

Dear Teddy,

My nose appears to be getting even bigger. I thought I had finally arrested its growth at the age of sixteen but the damn thing seems to have taken a new lease of life.

It's the snuff, you know. Pinching involves so much yanking and pulling that I am afraid I have unwittingly effected an enlargement. And another thing; it is beginning to veer to the right. There is a decided list which is not at all endearing. I am intending to abstain for a week in the hopes that everything will die down and return to normal, otherwise I will never get a girl.

At least I am getting stronger. Current examinations in the showers reveal certain anatomical developments. I have the potential, you know, for a magnificent chest. It just needs the right sort of encouragement which, at present, it is getting from all the sterling work I am putting in as a transport lad. Oh, I feel so good at the end of each shift! I experience such a sensation of worthiness and wellbeing. And what a release it is, those first few moments after we are let out of the cage on bank! You watch a shift coming out of the cage and rushing to the showers, and you will be struck by the number of smiling faces. People smiling just because they feel like smiling. Compare their faces to those of the men gathered at the heap about to begin their day's work.

For the most part I work with Geordie and Tony but on some shifts we are rearranged by the overman. I think Geordie and Tony are pleased with me as their marra. They could have done worse. I am not greedy and I do not make a fuss about "wet notes" every shift. Wet notes are worth 50p and in theory you are awarded them by a deputy or an overman whenever you have worked in wet conditions. In practice, wet notes are usually handed out as tips to lads for having worked extra hard. Some of the more greedy lads ask their deputy for a wet note at the end of almost every shift. Sometimes their persistence pays off, which only makes other lads start pleading, "If you've given him a wet note and I've worked just as hard as him, then I should get one too."

I'm not a crawler. Crawling does not just mean currying favour with your deputy, overman or whatever. It carries a host of other implications. A crawler is noticeably quick in obeying an order. Instead of carrying on with exactly what he was doing before the order and then complying after grumbling and muttering he actually replies to the official cheerfully and sets about his allotted task with enthusiasm. A crawler is a person who shows more respect to an official than to his own marras. He never answers back. He meekly accepts criticism from his boss and, of course, a crawler laughs at the overman's jokes when they are not funny. Naturally everybody is accused of crawling and I am no exception. Like most of the lads I feel it is childish to be rude without reason to the officials, a lot of whom are exceedingly good company. Nevertheless I would not go to the lengths of Benny Martin who used to sit next to our shift overman, Colin Turnbull, in the pit bus until we started teasing him about it.

Then, when somebody discovered that Benny Martin was the only one out of all the transport lads in our shift being paid Grade B, the teasing became more serious. No one was prepared to admit that Benny deserved the preferential treatment although, to be honest, he was the most hard-working and most capable of us all. No! Up went the cry, "You crawled for your wage rise."

"No, I didn't. I deserved it. I'm a bloody hard worker."

"Howay! You're a greedy, idle, crawling cunt!"

Above all, I am not assertive. Whenever anything has to be done I automatically take a back seat. It makes me easy to work with. Take yesterday for example. Geordie, Tony and I were putting some tension back on an endless rope that was slack. The job seemed complicated to me. It entailed using a sylvester (a tool consisting of a steel comb, a lever and two chains). I helped by shining my cap-lamp in the right sort of places while my marras did the work. If it had been anybody else there would have been grumbles about him not pulling his weight but, as it was me, it was taken for granted. There seems to be an unspoken agreement that I am excused semi-skilled labour because I just get in the way. I try my best, but I am hopeless. I am only good for humping girders.

Another problem is that I am short on stamina. This is quite a drawback. The other day Benny Martin and I were standing on a tram and trying to bolt the end of a bull (a long heavy girder) on to a clip on the roof girder. Benny suddenly dropped his shifter with which he was tightening the nuts on the clip. So, having asked me whether I thought I was strong enough to keep the bull up against my shoulder by myself for a few seconds, he jumped down from the tram to retrieve it. For the first couple of moments the weight was bearable, then my legs began to wobble. Very soon a huge weakness overcame me. It was a vast "I give up" feeling. Benny clambered back on to the tram and took his share of the weight just in time. I had the necessary muscle to hold the bull up but I lacked the stamina to keep it up for more than a few seconds.

I have noticed how lads with stamina also seem to have powerful characters. Each squad of transport lads, team of development workers, gang of waylayers or whatever has its unelected but natural leaders who take most of the decisions for the group throughout the shift. You cannot consult an official every time you want to do something. Somebody in the group has got to decide and that person is called the Number One. It is openly acknowledged. Quite often I have been asked, "Who's Number One in your squad?" and I say "Geordie Stephenson" or "Tony Davis". They are a recognizable type in the pit. They are people with stamina.

If a tram is derailed and you have tried to get it back on four different times using three different methods, and failed, the man with the qualities of a Number One will try a fifth time and a fourth method. Those not so determined will go in search of a deputy or another squad of transport lads to help them out.

A Number One can work and talk at the same time. That is not as easy as it sounds. The last thing you feel like doing when you are straining under the weight of a girder is to let fly with patter. I can flourish at the beginning of the shift and at bait time but while I work I like to keep quiet. Even in the days when I was trying to cut a figure down the pit, my liveliness always trailed off by the end of the shift, and if it happened to be a "rough un", I became monosyllabic. It's exactly the feeling you get at 4.30 a.m. at a debutante's ball. The wit has long since ceased to sparkle and all you sincerely want is for the bloody thing to finish so that you can get some sleep.

My lack of stamina makes me want to sit down whenever I get the chance. I cannot see the point of standing around doing nothing when you can just as well sit down and do nothing. During every shift there are times when nothing is done and it is in those brief intervals that I like to arrange myself comfortably on a chocknob or a stonedust bag. It is not just that I find the sitting more restful, it is also that I believe it to be the most efficient way of getting the strength to seep back into my spine. My theories of stamina conservation, however, are not taken all that seriously by the officials, especially not by shift overman, Colin Turnbull, who says that he does not know how tall I am because he has never seen me on my feet.

I am surrounded by people who all think they know best. None of them likes to be ordered around by anybody else. They all want to take the decisions and, just because somebody else happens to have that elusive quality which sets him apart as a natural Number One, it does not stop the rest of the squad getting frustrated.

110

Even I find it annoying sometimes that I am always being ordered about and never doing any ordering myself.

Sometimes you get two Number Ones working on the same squad. When they take different points of view about the best course of action you can get bogged down in endless discussions which are likely to develop into arguments. Then tempers are lost. Working with my two marras, Geordie Stephenson and Tony Davis, however, is a civilized affair. They discuss a thing nicely between themselves and even, on occasion, seek my opinion which they invariably ignore. But it is nice to be asked.

You see, I am never any trouble. I am not easily offended and I do not mind much if I am shouted at. I'll certainly never make it as a leader. But at least I've learned how to survive.

Yours, Kit

PS: Six days to go before jug.

Letter 23

Dear Teddy,

D-Day came and went yesterday and nothing happened. I was half expecting a posse of policemen to be waiting to collect me as I stepped out of the cage on bank. Geordie Smith told me that that was the normal procedure. They have had wanted men in the pit before.

The lads offered to have a "whip round" to help me pay the fine but I told them I couldn't possibly take the money and anyway I still had no intention of paying. I am constantly surprised by how suddenly this community can be so generous. It is even more astonishing when you consider how rough and offhand their relations normally are with one another. But the thing to remember is that the pit is a community and so people chip in and help out. If you want anything repaired for cost price like your car, your watch, your television or if you want to buy something cheap like a double bed or a kennel — no matter how unusual the need, there will invariably be somebody who can help. Of the four lodgings I have stayed in so far, the addresses of two were given to me at work. I have had my third watch repaired by powerloader John the Pole whose son's best friend is a jeweller. It cost me £1 instead of £3 or £4. I have received gifts of clothes from Geordie Stephenson, Bob Thomas, Ned Hawke and my last landlady. Actually Geordie was the most generous. He gave me about fifty pounds' worth of shirts. He would not take a penny off me in return, so instead I bought his wife a £10 bouquet. That's what being marras is all about. It means sharing your bait if one of you has left his up on bank, being able to shout at one another without fear of losing one's temper and sitting next to each other on the manset. It also means soaping one another's backs in the showers and telling one another quietly in the pub to rub the coal mascara out of one's eyes.

Of course an old-timer like Ned Hawke is not impressed. "It was far better in the old days when you had a decent chance of being killed. Now they don't give a damn. It's each man for himself."

But even Ned could not dispute the fact that there still remain some touches of consideration which demonstrate how caring the society of the pit can be. The week that a pitman working at Westoe dies, 10p is docked off the wage of each of the two thousand employees at the colliery and a present of the money is made to his widow. Once or twice I have seen thank-you letters pinned up on the colliery noticeboard from grateful widows. An annual sports day is organized for the children of the pitmen. The union looks after you if you are in trouble with the management and sees that you are dealt with fairly. Lord Wilberforce, in his 1972 Government Report on the miners, expressed astonishment to find that everybody, from datal lad to powerloader, got the same holiday money. This, he thought, was an extraordinary example of generosity on the part of the powerloaders who, after all, run the union. I remember being surprised by powerloader Hughie Ballon's reaction to my idea of making the pits more efficient by giving the ownership of them to the pitmen. He said, "What happens to people like Dougal? They will be the first people to get kicked out in your system for not pulling their weight."

Dougal is a simpleton. He wears his helmet the wrong way round. There are a number of miners like Dougal employed in the pit. They are given simple back bye jobs and are always under the supervision of older pitmen.

Nevertheless, I would certainly not like to encourage too kind a view of society down the pit. I have never known such a place for slandering, gossiping, carping and back-biting. They even have a special word for it, "calling". There is nothing Geordie Smith likes to do better than stir things up between marras. The other day he came up to Geordie Stephenson and said, "Hey Geordie man, Chris has been calling you worse than shite. He says you've got right bad taste. Those shirts you gave him, he says they are only fit to polish furniture with."

That was all in fun. The real mean stuff happens behind your back. God knows what is being said about me. I can just hear the phrases roll off the tongue, "The thing I can't stand about Chris is . . .", "What really gets up my nose about Chris is . . .", "Granted I'm not the world's most . . . but Chris takes the biscuit". Everybody gets a dose. It is as well not to overhear it.

Bubbling is pretty common practice as well. It means informing. As with everything down here, it is mostly done in fun, although it was quite serious the other day when Stevie Murpha told officials that it was Lamb and not he who had committed a certain offence. "Sure I bubbled. I'm hardly going to take the rap for something I didn't do, especially for a cunt like him," Murpha explained to me.

Of course, none of us owns up to anything. So if nobody is bubbling there is no way an overman or a deputy will find out who is to blame for any given incident.

Yours, Kit

Letter 24

Dear Teddy,

Well, I've done it! I tell you, I've done it! I got my rocks off! At long living last! Penetrating a vagina last night and leaving a deposit of Fraser sperm means that I have severed my last link with boyhood. I am now a man.

Mind you, I'm not going to say I don't deserve my success. I have spent months studying my quarry. Long gone are my tweed jacket, my lop-sided hair-cut, my Oxford bags and my lace-up shoes. The Tyneside Casanova model sports well-groomed hair, a tight shirt, a short jacket with a zipper, flared dress jeans and leather boots. A medallion round the neck is an optional extra but an earring is essential. Tattoos and scars, which help to harden the image, I'm afraid I cannot manage.

I have been going to the discotheque regularly and, after a number of visits, I have worked out my theory about how to "tap up a bird", as they say here. Once you are in the discotheque it is advisable first to team up with another lad because trying to tap up a lass by yourself is not conducive to success. It shows that you are not one of the lads and, if you are not one of the lads, then you must be one of the nerds. Furthermore, there is a practical reason why it is best to hunt in twos. The "loose fanny" (the unattached lasses) go around in pairs. So you have got to have somebody to dance with

116

the lass's girlfriend. The lasses show their availability by dancing round their handbags on the disco floor. The unattached lads stand on the perimeter watching. Occasionally a lad will turn to his mate and mutter, "OK, you take the one on the left." The lads then saunter across and engage the lasses in a dance. I used to make the big mistake of actually asking the lasses to dance and, on the rare occasions when I was accepted, I compounded my strategic error by continuing to talk to them. What a berk I was! Now I know better. I just give them a sullen macho stare and say nothing. That's the way to attract girls here in South Shields.

I suppose people are trying to communicate sex appeal and you can do that without saying anything. You just dish out a bit of body language instead. The patter you deliver at a later stage; after you have kept her interest for three or four records, jerked your head in the direction of the bar, offered her a port and lime and got her sat down between you and a wall so she can't escape. Given the slightest chance the lasses up here will reach for their handbags and bolt for the toilet.

Last night I spent another silent vigil glaring at lasses, buying them vodkas and trying to prevent them going to the toilet when in the end, after I had given up hope for the evening, I hit the jackpot. I had plonked myself down on a chair and was idly watching the dancing when a lass asked me for a light. We started talking. She was generous both in her physique and in her character. We were still talking twenty minutes later when the management cleared us out of the discotheque. We were getting on very well. I made her laugh and her eyes were all sparkly. It seemed a pity to go our separate ways home so soon after we had discovered one another.

It was gently raining and I suggested she come back to my place for a cup of coffee. She said she didn't like to because she had only just met me. I assured her that it was perfectly all right and soon we were dashing through the rain back to my lodgings. We took our shoes off, tiptoed past my landlady's room, and then along the corridor to my room where we sat on the bed and kissed one another. After a while I managed to get her into bed but she absolutely refused point blank to take off her dress. So with a minimum of foreplay and with a penis that obstinately refused to fully erect, I penetrated the lass and after a series of hurried little thrusts had an ejaculation of sorts. I then rolled over and stayed awake most of the night wondering why I didn't feel terrific. This morning I escorted her out of the house at about five o'clock and waved goodbye to her.

I can't wait for Monday to tell all the lads down the pit about it.

Yours, Kit

Letter 25

Dear Teddy,

I see from your letter that you find my tone, when discussing the fairer sex, smacking of immaturity and chauvinism. Well, of course, I am immature in these matters. I have had no experience, or at least almost no experience. And as for this accusation about chauvinism, you should hear them down the pit. And what excuse have they got? By all accounts these lads have massive experience. Benny Martin said he lost his virginity at the age of ten in a tent.

We talk about sex all the time down the pit. Lack of accommodation seems to make venues for premarital sex quite imaginative. It seems to happen almost everywhere except in a bed. The beach is a favourite place, cars come in handy and having a quick one on the settee in the lounge after the parents have gone to bed is, I am told, risky but warm. I have heard how many a lass in South Shields has been "shagged" standing up against a wall. The amazing sexual acrobat, Benny Martin, claims to have had a lass on top of a bus shelter. He had another on a slag heap. The best story of this kind I ever heard was about the time a lad, it could have been Benny Martin, escorted his lass into a public telephone box, put her on the ledge, where the telephone directory is normally kept, and had his way with her while all the time he kept a look out of the steamed up window to

119

the left and she made sure no one was coming from the right.

Sex! They give the impression they do it with anybody. I have been repeatedly urged by well-meaning mates to seduce my landlady who is a little under sixty years old. They say that if she drops her knickers, it will not be long before she drops her rent as well.

In matters of sex, according to them in their more outrageous moments, you can do no wrong as long as you avoid contact with animals, immediate relations and members of your own sex. But that leaves you a lot of scope. You are admired for making love to your best friend's girlfriend, somebody else's wife, your landlady, your first cousin, your aunt, a girl under the age of consent and a pensioner over it.

Sex amounts to an obsession. They love talking about it and, when there is nobody to talk to, they enjoy thinking about it. Benny Martin* tells me he thinks about it every quarter of an hour.

There are endless discussions about sex, from the best technique, to graphic descriptions of last night's "bonk". The interest in these stories lies not in how a lass with such a character and such looks and under such circumstances ever came to sleep with the narrator. What happened, that is what people want to know. So you get people like Benny Martin referring to the heroine as "it" because the woman is just a prop for the hero of the story. I have often heard a lad ask impatiently

*He is now in prison for sexually assaulting his sister-in-law.

120

as the story appears to meander, "Well, did you shag it or didn't you?"

There is no sexual deviation that I can imagine that I have not heard about down the pit. There is the "golden shower" — the idea of this perversion is to give your partner a piggy-back ride while she urinates over you. They talk about oral sex, tit-fucking, armpit-screwing, bondage, sodomy, blood-sucking and flagellation.

Imaginations are stimulated by an abundance of pornographic magazines. Electricians, fitters and button lads are especially partial to these magazines because they have so much time on their hands.

A change of subject is in order . . . I went to my first lodge meeting last Sunday. There were almost more people on the platform than on the floor. They look terribly crammed for space on the platform, whereas we on the floor were surrounded by empty chairs. In all there were about forty people, comprising fifteen committee members and twenty-five others.

Everybody was well-dressed and one sensed that this, in a way, has replaced the ritual of going to church for these people. The session cuts up the morning. The same effort is involved — having to get up at a certain time, wash, shave and dress in a Sunday suit.

Most of the meeting consisted of a discussion about showers. One man complained that you could stand for ten minutes in some of them and still not get wet: the water just sprayed all around you like an umbrella. As for the new experimental showers that the Lodge had pressurized the management into installing — they were downright dangerous. The water came out so fast that it near enough drilled a hole in your head. He had met lads stumbling around the shower room in a state of shock. A resolution was passed that the Lodge should press the management to have the showers numbered so that when somebody complained about a shower, he could refer to it by number. Frankly, by the end of the meeting I was disappointed. I was expecting to be harangued by red-hot subversives and told to go out and convert my fellow miners to the socialist cause. I wanted stuff about the overthrow of the capitalist system. I hadn't come to hear about replacing the old showers. No one called anybody "Brother". These Lodge committee members are good, solid men. They look and sound far more like town councillors than communist revolutionaries.

Yours, Kit

Letter 26

Dear Teddy,

Somebody got killed this week. A dozen or so men had hitched a lift at the end of a shift on a returning tram. Somehow the tram's clip (a metal contraption used to connect tram to haulage rope) had come disconnected from the rope and unfortunately the rails along which they were travelling were on the downward gradient. At first the miners did not notice but as the tram gathered pace they realized something was wrong. Unfortunately there was not time for everybody to jump off immediately. In a matter of seconds the tram was hurtling down the tunnel. A moment later it crashed. The last remaining passenger was splattered all over the roof.

Being responsible for a tram which runs away is the most awful experience for a miner. There is nothing he can do to stop it or to warn people to get out of its way, except perhaps flash his cap-lamp. It is no use shouting. The noise obliterates the loudest of bellows. As you run down the track to the tram's final destination you do not know whether you have killed somebody or not. Luckily I have never been responsible for a runaway tram — though one was nearly responsible for me.

Strolling from my button, twenty yards up an incline, I heard it. The rumble. Then I saw it. Like a rogue elephant on wheels it thundered down, pounding along the rails until it crashed into a protective girder, the impact of which sent its front wheels bouncing. I had not panicked because I felt safe as I was on the other side of the obstruction. But the sight and the noise of that runaway tram made a deep impression on me. Even though it was empty, in barely four seconds of freewheeling down a slope it had gathered enough speed to kill.

A white-faced Stevie Murpha came running down to me. "Thank God you're not hurt!" he said. Apparently, when he had unclipped the tram, the wedges behind the wheels slipped out of place.

Over the last couple of shifts, since the death, we have been prepared for the visit of the Union Safety Committee. Practically all transport of materials has been suspended while officials deploy us transport lads to tidy up the district's roadways, an operation which entails disposing of unsightly salvage, cleaning up piles of loose materials and then stonedusting the area.

Every aspect of safety has been checked and double checked. Old tuggers with brakes that slip have been replaced by new tuggers. Refuge holes have been painted white so that they are more noticeable. Dicky points on the tram track have been mended. Safety ropes are now on all the bulls. Safety rules have been printed on to sheets and pasted on to boards and hung throughout the pit. It seems a bit pointless doing all this after the accident, but it improves morale.

Yours, Kit

PS: I have been greatly honoured by Tony Davis. He

has invited me to have Sunday lunch with him at his home. People very rarely go to one another's homes. The social meeting ground is normally the pub. By the way, the saga about the non-payment of my £50 fine seems to have entirely petered out. I was sent another demand, this time in red ink, giving me a further seven days in which to pay. That period too has gone by. Still nothing.

Letter 27

Dear Teddy,

I really enjoyed Sunday lunch with Tony and his wife, Vivian. First Tony and I met for a few pints in the pub and then, at two o'clock, we went back for our lunch. His wife had made us a good meal but she must already have eaten because there were only two places set at the kitchen table.

After lunch, or dinner as they call it, we moved next door into the lounge and sat down with our coffee. Tony then showed me the present he has bought his three-year-old child — a set of general-knowledge books — and a family photograph album. All the time the colour television was on, with the volume turned down.

I felt content here, enjoying this easy domestic scene. It was a pleasant contrast to the racket of the world outside with everybody asserting himself — down the pit, in the pub and out on the street. Vivian said it was about time I got myself settled with a good Geordie lass. I made a suitably evasive reply and turned the question back on her by asking her what it was like to be married. She complained of loneliness. While Tony was out at work she had to stay in her home all day long, only ever stepping out to the shops. She was worried that she was becoming actually scared of the outside world because she was now so unused to it. She felt stranded, all alone with her child in her home. Naturally she did not see any men, but now she hardly saw anybody of her own sex either. Once a week she would take Joanne to visit Tony's mother, Winnie, but that — apart from the infrequent night out on the town with Tony — was about the extent of her social life, she said.

As I watched Tony and Vivian playing with their child on the settee, I felt how much I liked them. Tony overcame his small size by building up his body through physical training and hard work. Now he looks sturdy and powerful. Vivian has managed to overcome an appalling upbringing as a battered child and has emerged unembittered, happy and balanced. When I look at them I feel inferior. I was amazed that they were a couple of years younger than I and yet they had already got married and had a child.

Tony and Vivian said that they had married for love but there had been other factors too, like Vivian being pregnant. Also Vivian was keen to leave her home as soon as possible and marriage seemed to be the only real means of escape.

The day before yesterday another aspect of pit tradition was revealed when I injured Peter Pino. I was throwing chocknobs on to a tram while he was arranging them into neat piles when one hit his finger, causing a lot of pain. Immediately the five other miners who were with us began arguing as to who should escort him to bank. I naturally said that as I had injured Pino I should. But the others said that the very fact I had injured him disqualified me. I might injure him again, one ventured. Another then said that Pino belonged to his squad and not ours so it was his squad's right to escort him. We insisted that, as both squads had been working together, we should take equal responsibility for Pino's injury and so we should all have an equal chance to take him out. In the end Pino was taken out by his first cousin, Geordie Smith.

You may be thinking that this quarrel is a heart-warming demonstration of the selfless Good Samaritan, but you would be wrong. An injured miner is in high demand for more earthly motives. The two colleagues who escort him from the pit are free for the rest of the shift and still get full pay. In miners' argot this is "a sharp louse" (early finish).

However, you are not paid a full shift for a sharp louse unless you have authorization from an official. You get that only if you are escorting an injured man or if you are taking gear out. Naturally there is fierce competition to bag any gear that is portable and in need of repair. So, should you stumble across a faulty dac, telephone box, pull lift or delta bar, the smart pitman hides it from other miners. You then inform the two marras in your squad and you will hopefully be granted a sharp louse.

It seems needless to give somebody a sharp louse to take out a broken bit of equipment when it can perfectly well be taken out at the end of the shift. The official reason is that you are not allowed to take materials in a manset (the trams designated for the miners not materials). You have got to travel with it in a material set and material sets run to the shaft at odd times in the middle of the shift. However, that rule is never really enforced. Basically people try and organize their sharp louses so that they catch an early manset and travel in comparative comfort.

You must remember that the pit is not just an underground factory. It is also a community in which, over the years, traditions have grown up. Speed and efficiency are sometimes excused in the practice of these traditions. For example, I was once tipped off by an electrician near the end of a shift that a dac had just broken down and needed to be taken to bank for repair. It was too late for that shift so I went and hid the dac, so I could take a sharp louse for my next shift.

Because you have your pay docked and you lose that shift's productivity bonus, for not completing your shift without a sharp louse, few skive that often. However, there are lads who give their tokens to somebody staying the full shift. He then hands in the absentee's token along with his own at the end of the shift. The management, of course, presumes from the time book that the absentee has done a full shift and so pays him accordingly.

There is no way of being caught handing in somebody else's token because nobody checks to see how many tokens, if any, you throw into the token tray as you come charging out of the cage. The risk is in leaving — because if you are stopped in the manset by a suspicious overman, you can get into a lot of trouble. After all, it is tantamount to theft — being paid for work you haven't done. Personally I reckon that the couple of extra hours you get free is not worth the worry of not knowing whether your overman has spotted you missing from his shift.

Friday afternoons are the most popular for unofficial

sharp louses. None of the lads likes to lose one of the two best nights of the week just because of work. You emerge from the 4 p.m. shift at midnight, too late to enjoy all but the last hour of a nightclub. You come out from the 2 p.m. shift at 10 p.m. and so you miss all but the last round of drinks at the pub.

It is the younger miners who mostly shirk shifts. The older pitmen tend to be more responsible. Their attitude was reflected in a recent tirade from machineman Eddie Robson: "You young lads, you're a bunch of idle bastards. You don't do a drop of work when you are here, which you hardly ever are, because you're always taking sharp louses. Me, I've only ever had three sharp louses in my bastard life and on two of those occasions I was fucking carried out!"

Yours, Kit

PS: I've discovered that somebody has surreptitiously paid my fine. I went to Leicester to find out. I can't believe the police paid it, but who else? Probably my brother, although he categorically denies it.

Letter 28

Dear Teddy,

The reason it has been such a long time since my last letter is partly because there has been a dearth of incidents and partly because the news, which I was preparing to spring on you, has come to nought.

For a few months now I have been planning to get myself transferred to another pit called Sacriston as I am bored with Westoe. I am not learning anything new at the moment and I feel stagnant. I'd like to work on the face here but, because of the extra pay, so does every other miner and there is a seven-year waiting-list. I was told that at Sacriston the seams are so thin that few miners are keen to work on them.

So I visited the Sacriston pit last Saturday. From South Shields it is a two-hour bus journey and when I arrived there was only a pumpman on bank. I asked him about the possibility of a transfer and how long it would take for me to get to the face. He said I would not have to wait more than two weeks before I got my face training. As for a transfer — no problem. He would ring up the pit manager right now. And he did. But the manager was not at home. So we sat in the lamproom talking.

"I gather that the seams here are a bit on the thin side," I said.

"Why, they're not too bad, mun. Oh aye, we've got one seam that's eighteen inches. But what about the others? We've got one that's bastard nearly two and a half feet high. Why you could do hand stands on that face," he said, encouragingly.

He elaborated by saying that eighteen inches was much higher than one imagined even if it was a little low for comfort. Every extra inch makes a difference and he considered two foot six inches to be quite roomy.

There is only one other pitman I have met who agrees with this view and that was my instructor at Westoe, Ned Hawke, who said that you soon get used to working in a thin seam. Indeed he reckoned that it was easier to shovel coal lying down than standing up.

During this last month, while I had thought that my transfer from Westoe to Sacriston was going to go through, I consciously allowed myself to be persuaded by what the Sacriston pumpman and Ned Hawke had to say about thin seams. Once, when I found myself alone in the digs, I went around with a foot ruler measuring furniture. There is a little table, lower than a writing desk but higher than a stool, which was the necessary eighteen inches' clearance. I crawled under and tried to imagine that its legs were pit props and its body was the roof. I did not feel too bad. And, just as the Sacriston pumpman said, the two-foot-six-inch-high kitchen table felt like a gymnasium.

The Sacriston pit manager, Mr Pollock, advised me to write to Mr Quinn, Head of Area Manpower at Team Valley, about my proposed transfer. Mr Quinn wrote back to me, refusing my request for a move, explaining enigmatically that it was "not in the interests of the Board".

I thought, "Bugger that!" and took the first available bus to Team Valley where I saw Mr Quinn and asked him to explain his letter.

It was too far to travel to work, he said, South Shields to Sacriston and then Sacriston to South Shields every day. I said I was prepared to find myself lodgings in Sacriston village. So he asked me a number of questions about why I wanted to work in Sacriston pit "of all places". I had previously prepared some sensible answers to the likely questions and so did not hesitate in my replies. Eventually he agreed to telephone Mr Pollock to arrange for him to interview me.

At that interview it did not take long for Mr Pollock to realize that I was unsuitable coalface material. Furthermore, as he pointed out, in the event of a vacancy cropping up at the pit he felt bound to give priority to those lads in the village of Sacriston who were unemployed at the moment. Also, he said, a newcomer to Sacriston pit would have to wait at least two years before he would get his face training.

On the bus journey back to South Shields, I began to feel relieved that my plans had been thwarted. Now I could allow myself to believe all the tales I had heard down the pit about how awful it was to work in a thin-seam coalface.

Quite a few men told me they had worked in seams so thin that there was not enough height in which to turn a filler's shovel, which admittedly has a broader blade than a normal one. It has been known for a man to crawl fifty yards along the face to his place of work, only to discover that his shovel is facing the wrong way up, with the result that he is forced to crawl all the way back to the mulligate just to turn his shovel over.

An electrician told me about the time he worked in a twelve-inch seam. I think he must have been a filler (coal shoveller) in those days. He said he was frightened whenever the roof fell in. But the most terrifying thing of all was when you got stuck between roof and floor, he said. Although the actual wall was twelve inches high, no matter how well positioned the props, the roof had a tendency to slope so that a yard or two back from the wall the gap between roof and floor might be reduced to ten inches.

There were fillers with chests deeper than that. Imagine, as I did, crawling along a twelve-inch-thick coalface on your stomach using your elbows and knees to propel you forward, then suddenly getting jammed. If, for example, the roof sagged another inch before help arrived, you could not be pulled out.

Yours, Kit

PS: You might be interested to know that Irish John left the pit a couple of weeks ago.

Letter 29

Dear Teddy,

Just when I had really given up hope that I was ever going to be involved in a strike, it has happened. I was crossing the pityard on my way to work on the nine in the morning shift when a surface loco driver asked me, "Are you NUM?"

"Yes."

"No work today."

"Why?"

"Strike."

"No! Really?"

"Yes."

"What's it about?"

"Don't know."

"You're having me on."

"Have it your own way."

Sure enough, the locker room was deserted except for a union official. The canteen was crowded and there was an air of fun and excitement, like an unexpected holiday. We felt that, as it was out of our control, we might as well sit back and enjoy it.

First I sloped off to the *Shields Gazette* and gave them the story of the strike. Then I joined my marras in the pub where we remained until closing time. After that I took some money out of the post office and wasted it on foolish bets on the horses.

The next day a great union meeting was held in the Westoe Mineworkers' Social Club's Armstrong Hall. Over a thousand attended. There was no room in the hall for anybody to sit. The union officials sat up on the platform, which on Friday and Saturday nights is used as a stage for cabaret acts. As I was standing right at the back I could hear the union speakers who used microphones but I could not hear any of the questions from the floor.

Both the lodge secretary, Jim Inskip, and the chairman, Walter Slater — whose name I always mix up with that of Slater Walker — gave speeches. Walter Slater's speech was the more effective because it was more graphic, direct and emotive. At one point he growled, "Nobody is going to push us around." He attacked the pit manager, who is relatively new to his job, with the words, "He's only been here eight months and look at all the trouble he has caused already."

Then he attacked the Durham area union secretary, Walter Malt, who apparently had refused to come and mediate between the protesting men and the pit manager until the strike had been called off.

"You might expect that sort of stubborn behaviour from the management," shouted Walter Slater, "but not from you own brothers in the union." There was a chorus of consent.

It had all begun during the Tuesday four in the afternoon shift when the undermanager told the K65 facemen to go and help out at K60 face. Their own coalface was at a standstill because the shearer had broken down. The men refused to obey. K60 face was way out of their cavil, they argued. Furthermore, it was not true to say that there was nothing to do at K65 face. There was a certain amount of clearing up and securing of the roof that could be done.

The undermanager reacted by threatening to dock their pay if they did not do as he said. The men retaliated by downing tools and walking out of the pit. At the end of the shift there was a meeting of men and union officials in the pit canteen (about 150 people) and, there and then, it was decided to come out on strike. The union officials saw the pit manager and asked him not to allow the undermanager to dock the pay of the eighteen protesting powerloaders. The manager said he would do nothing until the men were back at work. The union officials said that the men could not possibly go back to work if they were not being paid for the work at K65. The undermanager said they would not be paid for what they were doing unless they did the work he wanted them to do at K60. Result — deadlock.

In this meeting, however, Walter Slater said that though he personally felt that the K65 men had acted justifiably, they nevertheless had been precipitous. They could have done as the undermanager had ordered them, but under protest, and then the union would have been in a stronger position to deal with the management in question. As it was, pitmen were losing money, unnecessarily. His speech reflected the mood of the meeting exactly and the vote was almost unanimous to go back to work.

So we capitulated. The eighteen powerloaders who had been the cause of the fruitless strike have since had to put up with a lot of jibes. Consequently on the tram which we share with men from the K65 district there has been a lot of "Howay, get the fuck out of it. You're not sitting next to me. You and your pigheaded marras cost us two shifts last week."

Yours, Kit

Letter 30

Dear Teddy,

"Working down here is no way to earn a living," said Casey, "it's a way of life."

You will not be surprised to hear that I have known right from the start it is not my way of life. At no point during the year and a half I have been here have I seriously considered settling down as a coalminer for the rest of my days. Mind you, I do realize that I am turning my back on a proper meaningful life at the end of which I will be somebody worth knowing.

Pit work might be nothing like it was before mechanization, but it has still got a lot more meat on it than most other modern jobs.

The day I have enjoyed most — for the feelings of allegiance to the pit — was the Westoe and Harton Children's Sports Day a couple of weeks ago. The sun shone on the Westoe pitmen and their wives and children. I was by myself but that did not spoil my pleasure as I strolled about the playing fields meeting people I knew and being introduced to their wives. In the next-door field was a funfair with bumper cars and shooting alleys, and I treated a mate's child to a ride in the ghost train.

Normally dirty, cursing powerloaders were smartly dressed and talking politely. It made me laugh to hear one proud Dad turn to another and say: "Well, it looks like our little 'un against your little 'un in the finals," as if talking about a couple of prize whippets. Altogether it made me feel glad to be a Westoe pitman.

The colliery band played most of the afternoon, pit rescue teams gave demonstrations of their first-aid skills and five-a-side football teams competed. They had names like the K60 Sizzlers and the Top Landing Thunderers — which gave you an idea of their powers on the football field and where they came from in the pit. It was supposed to be a day for the "bairns" but the adults enjoyed it as much, even though no alcohol was being sold because of past trouble in the beer tent.

But that day was a brief interlude in a period of my life that I now wish to draw to a close. It has been gruelling, the last half year. I suppose I have just been holding out for the experience of a national strike — but it doesn't look as if one is going to transpire this year.

You see, I am tired and empty. I am just watching myself go through the motions of living without any longer feeling anything happening inside. I find myself smiling or laughing at somebody else's quip and really I would prefer to scream. I am bored of hearing about the three Fs: "fights, football and fanny". I am sick of stories. If ever the talk wanders into the abstract it peters out altogether, deteriorates into a loud exchange of assertions, or else somebody comes barging in with an anecdote. You have even got to tailor your vocabulary or it is jumped on for being pretentious.

I remember one time with a lad called Bob Thomas. We were looking for an empty manset compartment. I pulled back one set of curtains and shouted: "Here, this one is unoccupied."

"Unoccupied?" bellowed Bob. "I suppose you mean — no cunt in!"

It is the noise I am fed up with: all the talking and laughing and shouting. I want to block my ears. I want peace. The only escape I have is my room where I can read some decent books. But even that is frowned upon. I should be watching the television or going to the pub like everybody else. One time my fellow lodger of these (my fourth) digs said to me: "What do you do in your room all day?"

"I read."

"Like hell. You have either got a woman in there or an inflatable doll?"

Did you hear that I cut short my Christmas holidays because I could not face another moment's socializing? You know what it is like up at Moniack between Christmas and Hogmanay — everybody up from London for a barrage of drinks parties and dinner parties and balls. I only just made it to Christmas Day. My nerve was going all week. I felt like a stranger in my own family with a smile stretched on my face and a clamp on my brain. All my brothers and sisters were back home for their precious ten-day Christmas holidays, trying to get as much as they could out of one another. But there was nothing for them to get out of me. I just couldn't sustain conversation and the family pretended not to notice.

On the night of 27 December, the evening before the Northern Meeting Ball, I sat up by myself after everybody had gone to bed. It was quiet and I was smoking. I started to feel very sorry for myself, which was enjoyable. So I lit a fourth and fifth cigarette. At last I got up and went upstairs to my parents' bedroom. I knocked the door, stepped inside and said I was going to South Shields the next day. My mother told me to climb up on their double bed and lie down beside them. So I lay there — twenty-five years old, thirteen stone, a Westoe coalminer, crying like a baby.

Early next morning my brother Rory drove me to the station. I have been back in South Shields for about a week now and my landlady isn't talking to me because I haven't been to work. I just sit in my bedroom and go for occasional walks.

My one comfort is that I now realize why I am so unhappy. The most valuable thing I have learned from my experience down the pit is how completely dependent I am on other people for my own sense of wellbeing. Previously I had thought that happiness lay in the satisfaction of all my appetites — sexual, spiritual, intellectual, social and emotional. Now I realize that it is unlikely all these different, occasionally contradictory, appetites can be met at any one time. Meanwhile, I need a person or people to whom I can open my mind and heart. To find friendship here I have had to suppress at least half of myself — the half that has been developed by my education and background. That side of me now needs some form of reciprocation because without it, I remain isolated and alone.

Having at last got through it I am not going to say I regret my eighteen months as a miner. Any time done, especially if it has been rough, you invariably feel has done you good. I suppose I have found out the importance of belonging. I don't belong here and I never will. It is pointless to prolong what has now become quite painful. So tomorrow I hang up my boots, pay off my landlady and take the train home to snow-muffled Moniack. I will rest and read and when spring comes I think I will take up gardening.

Yours, as ever, Kit

Postscript

Kit Fraser returned to Moniack that winter of 1979. He did not, however, take up gardening. He enrolled at Bristol University and took an honours degree in Politics in 1982. He recently married and is currently working as the sales manager of a Highland wine company, situated in the family castle.